The Perfect Bundle For Raising an Explosive Child

Positive Parenting Strategies for Raising an ADHD Child and Teaching Them Life Skills for The Emotional World Ahead

Kenneth Harvey

© Copyright 2022 - All rights reserved.

The content contained within this book may not be reproduced, duplicated, or transmitted without direct written permission from the author or the publisher.

Under no circumstances will any blame or legal responsibility be held against the publisher, or author, for any damages, reparation, or monetary loss due to the information contained within this book, either directly or indirectly.

Legal Notice:

This book is copyright protected, and it is only for personal use. You cannot amend, distribute, sell, use, quote, or paraphrase any part, or the content within this book, without the consent of the author or publisher.

Disclaimer Notice:

Please note the information contained within this document is for educational and entertainment purposes only. All effort has been executed to present accurate, up-to-date, reliable, and complete information. No warranties of any kind are declared or implied. Readers acknowledge that the author is not engaged in rendering legal, financial, medical, or professional advice. The content within this book has been derived from various sources. Please consult a licensed professional before attempting any techniques outlined in this book.

By reading this document, the reader agrees that under no circumstances is the author responsible for any losses, direct or indirect, that are incurred as a result of the use of the information contained within this document, including, but not limited to, errors, omissions, or inaccuracies.

I Dedicate These Books To My Daughter Who Has Opened My Mind To Learning More About ADHD And Encouraging Me To Write This Book To Help Other Parents Struggling To Understand ADHD

Contents

ADHD Raising an Explosive Child With a Fast Mind — 1

Introduction — 2

1. What is ADHD? — 7
   What Is ADHD?
   Causes
   The ADHD Brain
   Types

2. Conditions Associated With ADHD — 23
   Behavioral Conditions
   Learning Disorders
   Mental Health
   Physical Health
   Intensity Of Emotions: Common Causes of "Blowing Up"
   Management Techniques
   Managing With New School Challenges
   What We Can Do

3. ADHD and Emotion Control   52
    The Immediate Steps
    Discipline In the Face of a Meltdown
    Strategies For Emotional Balance Through the Day
    Being Gentle With Yourself

4. Good or Bad Disciplines?   65
    What To Do Before You Use a New Method
    Your Role
    Behaviors Outside Your Child's Control
    Different Strategies
    Extra Tips

5. Burn That Energy With Activities   76
    Dance Parties
    A Scavenger Hunt
    Create A Course With Common Items
    Get a Balance Board
    Playing Ball... With Balloons
    Inside Friendly Toys That You Don't Normally Think About
    Group Activities
    Solo Sports
    Trampoline
    Knock Out Some Chores
    Water Fight
    Yoga
    Let it Fly

      Sculptures
      Art
      Take Advantage of Things In Your Community
      Concentration Based Activities
      Older Kids

6. Nutrition and Well-Being   90
      The Why and the How
      MyPlate
      Foods To Focus On
      Foods That Your Child Should Avoid
      Sample Diet and Best Tips

7. ADHD Is a Superpower   110
      Benefits
      How to Make the Most Out of This
      Celebrities

8. Teaching Your Child Life Skills   125
      Activities and Strategies That Can Help
      Teenage Based Strategies
      The Skills

Conclusion   135

Life Skills For Your ADHD Teen   139

Introduction   141

Chapter one   147
Self Care and Grooming
    General Hygiene Tips and Tricks

What Problems Might Be Causing the Issue?
Having a Set Schedule
Additional Steps and Tips

Chapter Two 161
Keeping Them Healthy
  Diet
  Exercise
  Cooking

Chapter Three 191
Keeping On Top Of Those Emotions
  Why Does This Happen?
  Stress
  Anxiety
  Anger
  Strategies For Dealing With These Emotions

Chapter Four 207
Time Management and Organization Skills
  Time Management
  Organization Tips For ADHD

Chapter Five 225
Money Management
  Get Them The Proper Supplies
  Let Them Get A Job
  Guide Your Teen In Creating Their First Budget
  Talk To Them About Long-Term Goals
  Explaining Debt

Subscriptions
Natural Consequences

Chapter Six   237
At Home Maintenance
- "Life Hacks" That Can Help Those Who Have ADHD
- Easy Make Appliances
- Life Paperwork
- What To Do With All Of This Information?
- Clean Homes

Chapter Seven   253
I Can't Remember
- Some General Memory Tricks
- Exercises For The Memory
- ADHD Study Tips

Chapter Eight   269
Building Confidence and Social Skills
- Tips For Developing Social Skills In Teens
- Tips To Help Your Teen Boost Self Esteem

Review   279

Free Gift   281

Conclusion   283

References   285

ADHD Raising an Explosive Child With a Fast Mind

With strategies for emotional control and positive parenting to make your child feel loved

Kenneth Harvey

Introduction

I closed my eyes for a moment, trying to take a deep breath and calm down. I could hear my daughter sobbing as she shoved her spelling practice away from her for the fifth time. The critiques of others were playing in my head. It wouldn't take an average child more than 20 minutes to go over a spelling test, yet we were closing in on an hour.

When my eyes opened, I found my daughter looking at me. I could see the hurt and the frustration in her eyes. She wasn't acting this way because she "just didn't want to do her homework" or thought that she would get out of what we were trying to do by misbehaving.

She was genuinely frustrated with the situation. I sat there and tried to get her back on task. I tried to redirect her attention and finish the homework before us, but it wasn't working. I tried all of the methods people said would help all of the kids, but it wasn't helping mine. Why was this happening? Was my daughter a bad kid? Was I a bad parent?

The answer to both is no.

There was something else that was creating this problem. My daughter has always been wonderful and talented. But, like so many children before her, she struggles with attention deficit hyperactivity disorder (ADHD). The methods I was using were built for children whose brain was considered typical for the average child, and my child's brain was built differently, so these methods were not registering with her.

How often have you looked at your child and watched as they just seemed to blow up? It wasn't because of poor behavior, but rather, they seemed to be fighting their internal wiring. How often have you watched as your child reacted in a way that you didn't understand? Everyone around you tells you that they need more discipline or suggests things like corporal punishment.

The answer you get often comes with more questions that make matters worse. We are just starting to understand what ADHD entails, and doctors who diagnose are often not on top of new information because they have so many conditions to keep up with. Instead of understanding what's going on, you are left with explanations like "they just can't sit still," "they're really disruptive," or "they need more discipline." None of this advice is helpful, and it doesn't help us raise children into successful adults.

The answers to your questions have emerged in some of the latest research. You probably want to know what is going on in your kiddo's brain that makes things more challenging for them, and you probably want to know why they struggle and how you can help them.

The answers that have been found can help you! They show you the ins and outs, and they give you a path that you can take your child on to help them grow into a unique and successful adult!

I want to help you learn what tools and techniques have been developed that help children with ADHD.

First, we are going to answer a core question that you might not have been able to understand yet. Next, we will take a look at conditions and emotional states that correlate with ADHD, as well as how they might impact your child.

Once we have the basics down, we can dive in on how best to help children through their emotions. Traditional methods of discipline might not work, so we will explore other methods that don't involve tears of frustration from you or your kiddo. If you're wondering what some good ways to reach them through their ADHD might be, or if you are wondering about medication, we're going to cover that too!

Because a big part of ADHD is having a lot of energy, we will be looking at healthy and appropriate outlets. With energetic outlets comes the need for nutrition. Did you know that some foods can be detrimental to someone who has ADHD? It can make things worse! But what are those foods?

The final things we will touch on are the areas where having ADHD is a magical thing. Having ADHD is labeled as having a learning disability, but really, it often just means that you don't learn or think the same way others do, and outside of a standardized environment, this can be beautiful.

It's hard to watch our kiddos struggle. There are many areas of life, especially as children, where the world isn't friendly to those with ADHD. Despite this, your kiddo can still enter the world equipped with life skills that help them be their best.

I have only ever wanted this for my daughter. I watched as she struggled with school and with managing her ADHD. I encountered problems at every turn, which wasn't my daughter's fault. Doctors didn't seem to have the answers that I was looking for. And why would they when the road to proper ADHD management and treatment is an oddly controversial one (spoiler alert: the correct answer depends on your kiddo).

To help my daughter, I sought out every new study, every class and seminar, and every possible technique that I could find. I spent a ton of time learning and trying different things to see what worked for my kiddo.

My goal is to gather all of my resources, and I hope to create a comprehensive book that can aid you in helping your young child become a successful and fantastic adult.

Now, a quick disclaimer here, each child is different. As such, one technique may work wonders, and another may not. Your friend may find something that works for them, but it does not affect your child. You might even have two kids under the same roof, and the same technique might have different effects.

ADHD affects each person differently. That's why this happens. The reason someone has ADHD is often that their brain's wires are different than the average person's...but two typical brains won't end up looking the same. By extension, two ADHD brains won't look quite the same either.

Our first chapter dives right into some of these differences. Sometimes the best thing to do is to gain knowledge on the issue before you face it head-on. Are you ready?

Chapter One

What is ADHD?

Truthfully, what is ADHD? Why is it so important to understand? Before we dive in, I want to answer that second question for you!

ADHD is, sadly, so fraught with stereotypes that it can be hard to get an accurate picture of what you're dealing with. Many people characterize it in odd, often misleading ways. Maybe it's that children with ADHD gaze out the window and don't pay attention. Perhaps you've heard the stereotype that they can't sit still. There is always the stereotype that they are just badly behaved.

Subsequently, some stereotypes become damaging to people with ADHD. People might say that those with ADHD are dumb when, in fact, ADHD does not affect intelligence. Some of the world's greatest minds are suspected of having had ADHD. When measures such as an IQ test are used, children with ADHD score all over the map, just like children with typical brains do.

Another damaging stereotype that I hope to disprove with this book is that children with ADHD are just kids who need more discipline. Perhaps you've heard this from a judgmental relative or another adult in your child's life. I bring up these stereotypes because you won't be the only one to have heard them. Your kiddo will hear them too, and without the proper understanding, it may lead to the feeling that there is something intrinsically wrong with them when they don't have any control over their condition. Stereotypes like this might follow your child as they step out beyond your house, and with these strategies, you can act as a barrier to negativity.

Now for the question, you came here for!

What Is ADHD?

ADHD stands for attention deficit hyperactivity disorder. It was built upon the former moniker of attention deficit disorder (ADD), which became outdated around 1987. To date, it is one of the most common learning disabilities.

With its symptoms being more understood and some of the stigma starting to lift, more children are getting diagnosed. Today, just under one in ten children are diagnosed with ADHD (Parekh, 2017). Because we still do not know everything about ADHD, and we could still be missing some things, it's likely the numbers are a bit higher. To date, it's more easily identified in boys than in girls. Whether this is an actual gender difference or simply a lack of studies done on ADHD, the female mind is only now starting to be studied (Ellison, 2020).

ADHD is characterized by two main things: trouble paying attention and a tendency not to be able to sit still. As you might imagine, it's first identified when children reach school.

There are many treatments available for ADHD, and I will give a brief list here and give a lot more detail about these in later chapters.

One possible treatment is Cognitive Behavior Therapy (CBT), which is common for many mental disorders and learning disabilities. CBT is the use of specific strategies that focus on thought and behavior, which, in turn, leads to better emotional management. CBT can help with anger and stress management, which will go a long way in helping a child with ADHD.

CBT focuses solely on control of one's actions. This tends to be popular with more disruptive children as it can help them better understand what their behavior is doing and how they can change it.

When your child is diagnosed, you might be (or have been) recommended medications. Medications have varied effects. For some, medicine offers long-term relief, and there might be little to no relief for others.

For help in a child's support systems, there are options for classroom accommodations (Individual Education Plan (IEP), 504 plan, etc.) and opportunities for family therapy.

Finally, for parents, there are training sessions. Much of what we go over in this book are things I learned from attending many, many sessions so that I could help my daughter.

Causes

What exactly is the cause of ADHD? The short answer is that we don't know (yet). ADHD has to do with understanding how the brain is wired. Something that crosses one way in a typical brain will cross differently in the brain of someone who has ADHD. We are not sure what that something might be, although it's likely in the frontal lobe.

What we do know is that genetics can be a predictor of ADHD. As many as 75% of those with ADHD can point to someone else on the family tree who is equally diagnosed or exhibited symptoms.

While we try to study the exact origins of ADHD, we do have some previous work to rely on. Many things can happen to a person that can cause their brain to diverge from the typical path.

A lot of the answers may be in pregnancy. Smoking, drug use, and alcohol use have all contributed to congenital disabilities, including learning disabilities. Now, I am not here to point fingers at all! Many people do not realize they are pregnant, and all of the substances above are addicting. Without a solid reason, they may see no need to stop.

Another in-utero impact that can be totally out of our control is stress. If a pregnant person goes through job loss, housing struggles, a pandemic, or any event that causes a lot of stress during the pregnancy, that might impact the baby's development.

Another thing that can cause a brain to diverge from its developmental path is a brain injury. Now, there are some obvious causes of brain injury, like car crashes, for example. However, many other things can cause brain injuries, such as being dropped as a little one or having a lot of concussions as a kid. Any of these may cause altered connectivity in the brain.

Is there an increase in the diagnosis of ADHD? Yes. Does this mean that more kids have ADHD today than thirty or so years ago? Probably not, at least, not this much.

Our criteria are developing, so we are likely identifying children today who wouldn't have been in the 1980s. Adding to that, since we are starting to explore ADHD and its behaviors in girls more, there is a chance that diagnosis could rise to meet boys. There is a chance of overdiagnosis since we still don't know everything there is to know about the disease (this is why a second opinion is often suggested). In short, there isn't something out there that's causing an increase in diverging brains, just a better understanding of symptoms.

The ADHD Brain

What do we know about the brain's role in the creation of ADHD?

We don't know the exact answer, but we have it narrowed down. Currently, testing shows that the difference lies in the frontal lobe (American academy of child and adolescent psychiatry, 2017). It seems smaller and is potentially developing more slowly in children with ADHD. With this comes a chance that neural impulses aren't firing correctly or at a slower rate.

To think of our neural network, think of a telegram service. A message is sent over wires that connect to different parts of the brain and the body to tell those parts what to do. One of these messages comes in the form of the chemical dopamine, which those with ADHD seem to have a deficiency. Dopamine is essentially a motivation chemical. Without it, we wouldn't have any way to get out of bed. People with severe deficiencies can't move. Literally, if there is a fire next to them, without dopamine, the brain isn't sending them a signal telling them to move.

In a normally functioning frontal lobe, we see things like problem-solving abilities, and children develop this naturally as they grow. We also see impulse control, and the little voice in the back of our heads telling us not to yell at the person next to us is crucial.

Memory and language are a part of the frontal lobe. Memory is a function we may take for granted. For a child with ADHD, having a memory deficit can make schooling even more frustrating. The frontal lobe also controls our judgment and ability to delay gratification. So are our planning and decision-making abilities. Motivation, the ability to pay attention, and even social behavior seem to be rooted in the frontal lobe. They all require dopamine on some level as well.

Again, we are unsure what is happening but think of your child. How many areas do you think they are struggling within the categories we just mentioned?

The frontal lobe is the center for all of these things (the headquarters, if you will), and dopamine functions as the executor for making these functions happen.

It's hard to see your child act out, get in trouble at school, or do things that you and they know that they should not be doing. While our science hasn't been able to link ADHD to a specific cause, it has shown that ADHD isn't just a behavioral issue but a true brain deficit (one that, I stress, does not impact overall intelligence).

In the future, we are likely to discover a more specific answer as we continue to dig for one. In the meantime, the current research tells us that it isn't just about not paying attention, acting immaturely, or that there is more of a need for discipline. There is a cognitive reason behind everything.

This is the general process of ADHD in the brain for most people, but as I stated before, each person is different, and ADHD may look unique from one child to the next. There are three distinct categories, or types, of ADHD that we will look at next.

Types

I want to introduce you to three children.

Morgan is seven years old, and she's very excited to be going into second grade. Her mother, however, isn't nearly as ready for her daughter to enter this new step. In first grade, the activities were more mobile and fun. Her mother knew that second grade would step it up, and she wasn't sure Morgan was ready. The second grade would mean that Morgan would spend more time sitting still and listening to a teacher and less time with activities.

Morgan's teachers always described her as seeming to be in another world. She always seemed far away and did not pay attention to the lessons. If Morgan were sitting still, she would show signs of apparent boredom. She had a hard time staying on track and keeping her mind on one thing. New information always seemed more challenging for Morgan to grasp than it was for her peers. It was hard to get Morgan's attention, and it often did not seem like she was listening to her teachers. While Morgan never seemed to disrupt class, her teacher found that they constantly had to give her supplies to do her work with because Morgan would misplace hers. Morgan's diagnosis of ADHD wasn't a surprise to her teachers, but it was a surprise to her father, as Morgan was never in trouble or disruptive. She just seemed to be daydreaming most days.

When Morgan's classmate was diagnosed with ADHD two years before she was, no one was surprised. Jamison was a good kid, and even his teachers thought so. However, Jamison's mom always commented, "he just does bad things" in conferences. Jamison was known for being a little immature. While the rest of his classmates seemed capable of sitting still and doing what they were supposed to, Jamison would squirm, no matter what. His teachers asked him if he was uncomfortable, and he always said he was fine. Jamison was also prone to fidgeting with nearby objects. The tape that kept his name tag in place had nearly been ripped off at this point, which annoyed his teacher. Even if Jamison was supposed to be doing his work, his teacher found that he would fidget in his seat or play with little toys that he got from home.

Jamison always seemed to have his eye on the clock and asked when lunch and recess times were more than once each class. Jamison would get up from his seat and walk around the classroom more than any other student. Finally, he rarely raised his hand to answer a question, would talk out of turn, and disrupt others around him.

The last child I want to introduce you to is Eli. Eli was diagnosed with ADHD when he was five years old. Eli rarely paid attention to what his teachers were saying. It often seemed that anything the teacher told him would go in one ear and out the next. Teachers often had trouble getting Eli to complete his work. Eli would often respond that the work was boring when his parents asked about it, so he didn't want to do it. If Eli did his assignments, they would often go missing, and he wouldn't be able to turn them in. When group activities were happening, Eli often seemed as if he wasn't moving as fast as his classmates were.

Eli's teachers noticed that of their students, Eli usually had the most trouble in terms of understanding the information. If they slowed down quite a bit, they were usually able to help, but that made it hard to help other students.

Eli always had a restless air about him. His leg was always bouncing, and he seemed to consistently have something in his hands that he was fiddling with.

Eli often talked to his other classmates, even when the teacher was teaching. An additional worry that his teacher had was that Eli tended to yell at others or at things that were frustrating him, with little thought to the consequences of his actions.

Morgan, Jamison, and Eli have the same diagnosis: ADHD. Nevertheless, it seems to affect each of them in different ways. So far, there have been three identified types of ADHD.

Inattentive

With inattentive ADHD, you are not struggling as much with sitting still, speaking out of turn, or misbehaving. What ADHD is attacking is your attention. With inattentive ADHD, you might miss some of the small things or even obvious things to everyone else.

Distractions come upon you much harder than they might someone else. It's hard to maintain your interest in something, leading to you getting bored quickly.

When you try to focus on a task, you can't. Something seems to get in your way actively, interrupting your focus.

You struggle with having a cohesive thought structure in your brain. Your thoughts are all over the place and hard to get straight.

Learning new things is a strain too, and your brain may struggle to encode this information into your memory.

Daydreaming, or at least the appearance of daydreaming, is a common characteristic of this type of ADHD that can show up in slow movements, not paying attention or listening, and potentially not taking in any new information.

Equally, following directions is often a struggle for people with this type of ADHD.

Finally, you are more likely to lose and misplace things. For your kiddo, it might be pencils, paper, missing assignments, etc. For you, it might be things like your phone or your keys.

Inattentive ADHD is often less disruptive to the world, and because of this, it can be easily missed, especially in kids with above-average intelligence.

Let's say, for example, that your child is in kindergarten. They exhibit all of these symptoms. Your child's teacher watches as they seem not to be paying attention, and she is concerned.

But, your child is already aware of most or all of the concepts the teacher is talking about in the classroom. They finish the work quickly and do well. This alleviates the teacher's concerns and keeps the ADHD undetected. That's not to say ADHD can't be detected in children with above-average intelligence or that children diagnosed early with this type of ADHD have below-average intelligence. It shows us that a child's performance may not be an indicator of ADHD.

Can you guess which of the three children above have inattentive ADHD?

The answer is Morgan. Her actions are not disruptive to the environment around her, but they make it very hard for her to learn.

When girls are diagnosed with ADHD, it's often inattentive ADHD, which is harder to spot due to many scenarios like the one above.

Hyperactive-Impulsive ADHD

Hyperactive impulsiveness is often the basis for several stereotypes of ADHD, particularly those where the child acts out and is violent. This stereotype isn't accurate, but it's important to highlight that this type of ADHD is often spotted sooner because the symptoms tend to be more disruptive to everyday classroom activities.

Sitting in one place seems like it would be a nightmare to any child, but it is challenging for those with this type of ADHD. Maybe they are tapping their feet, drumming their fingers, disturbing the others near them, or messing around with a nearby object during a moment when they should be doing something else. They may even get up from their seats when they are not supposed to due to the difficulty they face sitting still for as long as school demands.

People with this type of ADHD tend to be chatterboxes. While there are many people out there who talk a lot, people with this ADHD have a hard time rearing themselves and giving others a chance to speak or knowing when to stop altogether. For example, a student might be trying to engage his classmates in conversation while the teacher is talking. Along with talking to others, you might hear notes that a student with this type of ADHD is good at participating but bad at taking their turn to do so. It's common for them to forego classroom etiquette, such as raising one's hand before giving out the answer. Additionally, they may make loud comments that are not in line with what is going on at that moment.

A person with this type of ADHD may have trouble reading, working on assignments, or participating in other activities requiring a person to be quietly engaged.

Some final notes on this ADHD form are that people with it tend to be impatient, impulsive, and always need to be doing something. Children, in particular, may have trouble waiting for their turn. They might try actions such as cutting in line or pushing other children out of the way. They may be "bouncing in their seat," so to speak. It's also common for children and adults with this type of ADHD to struggle with considering the consequences of their actions. This is a problem not just for those with ADHD but also afflicted by other frontal lobe deficits.

This form of ADHD, as you can see, is more disruptive to the world around them, and it's most common in boys as opposed to girls.

Of the three children above, Jamison has this form of ADHD. He shows hyperactivity, trouble with talking outside of appropriate moments, and difficulty following directions. This stood out very early on in his classroom behavior, and he was able to get a diagnosis and treatment early.

Combined-Type ADHD

People with combined-type ADHD have to fight both inattention and hyperactivity. You can probably already see where this might be going with that name.

Impaired with this type of ADHD, you are likely dealing with symptoms of inattentiveness. You might overlook the small things that everyone else sees. You might have trouble with focus. You might find yourself growing bored within seconds of beginning the task. In addition to this, staying on task might be challenging. Losing everyday items might be a common occurrence. There might be trouble when it comes to listening to instructions. To shorten the list, the attention span of someone with the combined type will suffer.

There will also be symptoms of hyperactive-impulsive ADHD. The trouble with sitting still and the fidgeting that comes with it will be there. There will be trouble with interruptions and talking when one isn't supposed to be.

Eli is our example of a person with a combined type of ADHD. A person doesn't have to have all of the ADHD symptoms in order to be considered as having combined-type ADHD, and they have to have a significant amount that roughly balances the two categories.

I want to highlight that it's highly unlikely that a child intends to be disruptive or not be paying attention or following instructions. It has to do with their brain not processing the proper signals, leading to these outcomes.

Perhaps you may have noticed this already or may not have. The brain is a complex system, and it's not uncommon for one area of the brain to have issues that create more than one problem. Several conditions seem to go hand in hand with ADHD. You may have already seen these diagnosed, be waiting on a diagnosis, suspect it, or your child may only have ADHD. The brain can be quite a spectrum.

Our next chapter will talk about some of these conditions and the emotions your child might be struggling with due to their ADHD. We'll also talk about what might impact school, which has become even more important with education often taking place in the home.

Chapter Two

Conditions Associated With ADHD

ADHD itself can feel like quite a challenge to manage, and for many of us, it isn't the only thing that we will be tackling.

The reason it's essential to understand where ADHD might come from in the brain is because it helps us better understand where some other issues might come into play. The frontal lobe is responsible for a lot, and with an ADHD diagnosis, it is thrown off balance.

Like many of you, I find myself tackling more than one challenge. In addition to ADHD, my daughter has autism. While this book is dedicated to ADHD, I have taken time to learn about both, and I understand that knowing what you can about all diagnoses is essential. With this in mind, I have created a list of some common conditions that come with ADHD to help you better understand how to treat them.

Behavioral Conditions

Few children intend to misbehave, but it is more common in children with ADHD due to the brain imbalance. As we talked about above, each brain can be different, and for some, the chemical signals that the brain sends are so strong that it creates another behavior disorder.

Oppositional Defiant Disorder

Oppositional Defiant Disorder (ODD) commonly starts before the age of eight or after twelve. It is a common behavioral diagnosis that often goes with ADHD.

If your child has ODD, you might notice that they often get angry. They are likely to disobey rules blatantly. If you request something from them, they will likely refuse to help or simply ignore you. If you have other children in the house, they may show resentment towards them. This resentment can also transfer to animals you have or other children they are close to. This can escalate into violence if they experience any flooding, particularly with angry emotions.

They may show signs of being annoyed at small things and make a strong habit of annoying others. It's also prevalent for someone with ODD to blame others for their behavior.

When this happens, especially in younger children, try to walk them through the events. Have them give their version of things that happened. It gives them a chance to explain their point of view and how they think the other person might be at fault. It allows you to point out what they might have done differently to avoid the situation entirely and how it might not be the other person's fault at all.

Every child is occasionally guilty of the behaviors above, but these behaviors will occur much more often for children with ODD.

It's also important to note that children with ODD are less likely to engage in these types of behaviors if they are more comfortable with the people they are with.

Many ADHD techniques that we discuss below will also provide a ton of help for ODD!

Conduct Disorder

Conduct disorder is a disregard for social norms to the extent that it is harmful to others. This doesn't mean shaving one's head, deciding to use different pronouns, or dressing in non-traditional ways. Conduct disorder outlines practices that, at their most serious, involve breaking the law and causing genuine harm to others. People with ADHD often do not think of the consequences they will face when they complete these acts. Instead, what they think of is that there is an adrenaline rush that comes with the action, which can make those with ADHD inclined to try them and prone to this disorder.

Serious violations of home rules can occur, including damaging property, getting angry and breaking out into fights, breaking rules that are vital to be upheld, and occasionally running away.

Most of these actions will not be premeditated, and they are a heat of the moment response to a surge of adrenaline or flooding.

Your child may also engage in acts of bullying and cause fights at school. They may also participate in lawbreaking acts such as stealing, robbery, speeding, and vandalism.

Conduct disorder often does require that a professional step in and help, but there are things that can be done about it.

Continuous accountability is one measure that prevents conduct disorder from becoming something that significantly impacts their life. Laying out consequences beforehand and having a visual aid can help too.

Another thing is allowing the natural consequences to play out. What do you do if your kiddo damages property around the home? Have them pay to fix it. This doesn't have to be a harsh consequence (you can still take a gentle tone), but it does create a cause-and-effect link.

Now, this understandably gets harder if your kiddo broke the law. One thing to remember is that children have their records expunged, so this won't be on their records permanently.

If they break the law, they might be counting on you to bail them out and keep them from facing trouble. Sadly, they have committed an action the court system wants them to answer for, and it's best to learn what can happen when you break the law when you are a child, as opposed to when you are an adult, and the consequences are much more severe.

Learning Disorders

Up next are learning disorders. These are particularly difficult, as having ADHD can already make learning difficult in a typical classroom setting. Below is a set that commonly goes with ADHD.

Dyslexia

Dyslexia affects a person's ability to read. Many have described letters changing shapes (For example, a 'd' turning into a 'b' or an 'm' becoming a 'w.') or the letters seeming to move around the page constantly. This one gets the most attention and representation, and public figures have mentioned struggling with it.

Many schools have programs that can help with dyslexia, and there are several online resources as well.

Dyscalculia

Dyscalculia affects math. Number computation may be easy for someone with a typically developed brain, but that center isn't developing so easily for others.

One important thing to remember is that many careers out there don't involve math. In fact, very few will require high levels of computation. Adults who struggle with math are still very successful.

In the meantime, though, check out those school resources. See what is offered online too!

Dysgraphia

Finally, there is difficulty in writing. Whereas some may have trouble reading, others may have trouble getting the words onto the page.

These have links to a frontal lobe malfunction, and it is possible to have all three. Typically when these issues appear, the best course of action is to create a plan involving the parents, teachers, consulting doctors and psychologists, and the child themselves, especially as they grow older. It does take time and patience, but these issues can often be overcome or compensated for.

Mental Health

Serotonin production is one of the brain chemicals believed to be imbalanced in a way that results in ADHD. The use of serotonin by our brain is widespread, and in addition to controlling the aspects that we see affected by ADHD, serotonin is directly linked to our brain's mental health and wellness. It is currently believed to be primarily involved with the two disorders listed below.

Depression

Depression has been a hot topic. We are seeing a massive increase in diagnoses across the world. It could be that we are better at recognizing it. It could be that we are over-diagnosing now or underdiagnosing in the past. It could be that the current circumstances have led to situations where people are more likely to feel depressed.

Depression, as stated above, is often found in people with ADHD. ADHD can interfere with one's quality of life. Children may feel as though things are not in their control because of their ADHD, including school, behaviors, interactions with others, and others' perceptions of them.

Does nearly every child experience symptoms of depression in their lifetime? Yes, but not at a consistent rate. Diagnostic criteria state that for someone to be diagnosed with clinical depression, they have to experience multiple symptoms of the disease. These symptoms need to be present for at least two weeks and need to have a significant impact on a person's ability to function every day. That being said, there are issues such as minor depressive disorder or high functioning depression, and it's a good idea to keep your eye out for these issues too!

For your child, this won't just be a brief period, and it will impact their ability to function in an entirely different way than ADHD would.

One thing to look out for is a strict sense of misery. That might seem like a lot but think about it. Does your child always seem to be sad or upset? Do they have hope or look forward to things?

This level of sadness and misery will seem so bad that it can make it hard to get out of bed. No matter what you do (Whether it's making their favorite cookie recipe or turning on a favorite show.), nothing seems to make the situation better.

Another core characteristic is that their normal favorite activities no longer interest them. They may engage half-heartedly, or their energy for the activity drains almost as soon as it is gained. Typically, a child with ADHD will focus heavily on activities they enjoy, so this change is very likely to stand out.

Focus and concentration symptoms can be hard to spot since your child faces these every day, but what have you noticed? Has your child seemed off lately? Has there been any sign of their ability to concentrate changing? Perhaps they have suddenly gotten bad grades in what was once their favorite subject. This is another sign of settling depression.

The final sign is a lack, or a devaluing, of their self-worth. Talking with your child about the importance of high self-worth and how they view themselves can act as a preventative measure for depression and help you spot the signs.

Depression is a severe issue. In fact, it can kill. It is best to always keep an eye out for signs in any children. An open dialogue of communication can go a long way. There are many treatment options available, and you should talk to your doctor if you think your child is showing signs, and they can walk you through the various treatment options.

Anxiety

Anxiety's relationship to serotonin is less known, but there is still a documented correlation.

Fear is a normal emotion, and worry is a normal emotion. What is not normal is for it to interfere with a person's daily functioning.

One type of anxiety is known as separation anxiety. Most children show hesitancy when separated from a familiar adult, but children with separation anxiety don't handle it well. They will try to run after the person in question. If that doesn't work, they are likely to resort to methods such as screaming, melting down, or even becoming violent. This behavior will commonly persist for at least a couple of weeks before it's considered to need a diagnosis. Children with separation anxiety are not likely to adjust to their new environment. They may not engage in other activities and may not even respond to the other adults in the room. Parents can work with teachers and daycare providers, and if it continues to be an ongoing problem, they can talk to the child's doctor.

Another type of anxiety disorder is social anxiety. Social anxiety comes into play with new places and new people.

Like separation anxiety, this fear does not just subside. Instead, it gets worse the longer the child is in the situation. There are several ways to combat this. You can try and tour new places when they are not busy or loud, so your child has a better sense of what to expect. You can introduce your children to new people on more comfortable grounds, such as asking to meet one on one with a teacher while you are in the room. With technology, this can become even easier. If strategies like this are not working, talk to your child's doctor about some other things you can try.

Finally, there is general anxiety. This one is often recognized as quite horrendous to those who have to experience it because it is harder to fight. Generalized anxiety does happen to everyone, but it's usually in a manner that is within a person's control. For example, even though you know a school test will be pretty easy and you know that you have studied it, you still experience that feeling of butterflies in your stomach. You are worried that you will fail; the difference is that this sense of failure will leave you after the test. It will not leave someone with generalized anxiety disorder. This constant sense of dread follows them, and they are worried that something terrible will happen even if there is no logical reason to believe it will. To combat generalized anxiety, you often have to dive into cognitive behavioral therapy practices.

Anxiety can place a burden on a mind that is already strained with ADHD. Keep an eye out for signs. Having strategies on hand can make a huge difference.

Physical Health

It is easy to overlook these things until something terrible happens. While it is technically a learning disability, ADHD puts children at a unique risk of physical harm.

Injury Risk

Children with ADHD have an increased risk of injury. Children lack coordination abilities which increases their risk of falling, but those with ADHD have an additional thing to worry about.

Think back to what you have learned about the frontal lobe. One of the things it is responsible for is logical thought. Another thing that it's responsible for is "if-then" thinking. A child without ADHD may logically think, "jumping out the window will hurt me." A child with ADHD, unless they have prior experience to pull from, would think, "jumping out the window looks like fun." The logical fact that they might injure themselves goes missing. With if-then thinking, a child without ADHD may say, "if I run into this busy street, I will likely get hit by a car." A child with ADHD may say, "dad is on the other side of the street, and I want to run to him." As you can imagine, that's likely to cause injury.

There is also the inattentive aspect of ADHD. A child might run through the street without even noticing that cars are on the road.

The hyperactive component is there too. A child might be running around quite a bit on the playground to burn energy, and they are more likely to fall and injure themselves. There is also a chance of developing dangerous and thrill-seeking behaviors in teens. A typical example is speeding.

To combat injury, many experts recommend always wearing proper safety gear, including helmets, knee and elbow pads, seatbelts, and anything else appropriate for the activity at hand. Suppose children engage in activities such as speeding or running into the road. In that case, some recommended steps are for a parent to be firm about the rules and draw up contracted consequences for breaking them (For example, losing the car if they are speeding.).

Staying Healthy

Specific issues may exacerbate ADHD symptoms, or ADHD may increase the risk of particular conditions.

One thing that can make ADHD a lot worse is not getting enough sleep. Our brains use a certain amount of energy and power during the day, and sleeping helps us gain this back and regenerate any neural connections that we might have lost during the day. When we don't get enough sleep, we are not giving our body enough of a chance to replenish that energy. Furthermore, it's not giving our brain a chance to regenerate those connections. Even without ADHD, this can be tough. You might have had the experience of being on autopilot all day or struggling to get through the next task.

As we discussed in the first chapter, people with ADHD are often operating with reduced frontal lobe capacity, where many neurons are attempting to make up some difference. Not getting enough sleep can make ADHD symptoms even worse as the brain hasn't had a chance to repair any neurons.

Another thing that can increase the expression of ADHD is the overuse of electronics. When you've been on your phone for an extended period, do you feel that sluggish feeling? For some reason, your energy is just gone. If you tried to do something now, you would likely run into many mental blocks. This is true for all children too. More and more experts say that time away from the screen is best because it impacts children's behavior. They are less attentive, more likely to misbehave or out of turn, and more likely to refuse or struggle to do things that make them bored. Sound familiar? Children with ADHD are likely to see an increase in these symptoms.

Finally, it's encouraged to have your children eat a balanced diet as a preventative measure. Having a healthy diet increases the outlook for all age groups. In children, it's essential to have as the brain develops, as it can aid in the creation of a healthy brain. This doesn't go both ways (ADHD is highly unlikely to be caused by a poor diet), but having a healthy diet can aid in the development of a healthier brain. Finally, children with ADHD seem to be more likely to develop weight conditions, which a balanced diet can help!

Intensity Of Emotions: Common Causes of "Blowing Up"

ADHD may have a lot of material things associated with it, but one of its most significant issues lies in the behavioral sector. You are probably wondering why your child is so prone to blowing up. Why is it that they experience these behaviors? If you are newer to ADHD parenting, what might you experience?

Flooding

Josh was outside playing with his siblings while his parents talked about his new diagnosis of ADHD. All of a sudden, they heard a cry. When they went outside, Josh was yelling at his younger brother, whom he had pushed. His younger brother was the one they had initially heard, but Josh was also in tears. His face was red as he yelled from being so upset. After a moment, his parents were able to get to the bottom of the situation. Josh's younger brother had been playing with a toy firetruck of Josh's, and he'd broken the ladder. While Josh's younger brother confirmed that he'd broken another toy of Josh's last week, it didn't seem enough to cause this sort of reaction, yet it did.

The reason for this is flooding. With ADHD, the brain doesn't always regulate properly. In this case, the reaction of anger flared up within Josh. For us, that pang might go away after a moment or two, but for someone with ADHD, this response can build and build and build until it becomes an all-out explosion. If your child seems to blow up at small things, this is likely a huge part of why. Working with them on managing extreme emotions can really help!

There is a reverse of this as well. Have you ever tried to use a fire starter, and no matter what you did, it just wouldn't light? The brain has this issue too. Something happens, and the emotional center of the brain signals and signals and signals, and it just... does nothing. The brain may not be able to start an indication of emotion at this point in time.

Criticism

Criticism can feel different to someone with ADHD. Imagine that you are 10-years-old and in an art contest. You finish your work and present it to the judges. "Blending these colors might help you achieve a more real and natural look, but overall it looks amazing!" is the feedback you get. Overall, you see it as positive. They said that your work looks great! That's a win! Someone with ADHD might not see it that way.

Someone with ADHD is in the same contest, and they receive the exact same criticism. Instead of taking the whole message away, they hyper-fixate on the first part. They head to their bench upset, thinking their art wasn't good enough. Even being placed in the top 10 might not be enough.

As they experience constructive critiques in school, activities, or the workplace, they are much more prone to latching onto these things and acting irrationally (Lashing out at the person who gave the critique, for example.) when it was a simple thing or even when the feedback is positive overall. If you are trying to prevent strong reactions, starting with and stressing the positives is often a good way. If you are trying to help them in the future, it might be best to try and help them with listening skills and emotional regulation.

Fear and Anxiety

Have you noticed that your kiddo doesn't want to go places like school or even hang out with others? This behavior can become so intense that they won't leave the house no matter what you do. You're worried about the level of social interaction they are getting (Surely it isn't enough, right?), and you want them to get out more. Yet, trying to get them out of the house has been proven to be a nightmare.

Fears surrounding social situations tend to be worse for someone with ADHD. Making a mistake, acting wrong, or not fitting in seems to be exaggerated, especially with ADHD. We already experience these emotions at a disproportionate level when we are teens, so having this issue can worsen the already crazy situation.

Denial

Anna's family has just been through a difficult time. Their family pet, a cat named Pumpkin, has just passed away. Anna adored Pumpkin and spent time with him every single day. When Pumpkin passed away, Anna's mom did the best she could by preparing a little funeral and giving Anna a chance to say goodbye to her pet. She hoped it would help Anna process, but it didn't seem to be working.

Anna would often come home and put cat food in Pumpkin's dish, then sit by it and do her homework like she used to. When Pumpkin inevitably didn't come, Anna would go outside and call his name until her mom told her she had to come in. Whenever her mom tried to talk to Anna about it, Anna seemed to deny that Pumpkin had even passed away, and she said that he was probably lost somewhere.

Anna's mom was growing concerned. She knew Anna had ADHD, but this didn't seem like a learning disability issue. Instead, it seemed like Anna denied reality.

That's exactly what Anna was doing. Many of us go through a denial phase in order to put off feeling our emotions for "just a little longer." However, with a brain affected by ADHD, flooding is a potential, especially in a situation like Anna's. So, it might be beneficial for her to remain in denial for as long as she can.

This phenomenon can translate to events that cause anger or stress as well.

If the problem persists, try to talk it out. In the case of Anna, her mother might sit down with her and talk about Pumpkin being gone and how it is okay to feel sad or angry. If it continues to be a problem, she might get a school counselor or another mental health professional to help.

Caught In a Storm

When things get intense, we often respond in one of two ways, and we either choose to stand our ground or flee the situation.

Our fight-or-flight response is essential in telling us when danger is around us. For example, if you are camping and see a bear a few feet away, you don't have time to think about the best course of action. So, your fight-or-flight response makes a quick decision. You either fight (or stand your ground and hope you aren't seen as food) or run.

For someone with ADHD, situations that cause even a minor amount of stress can quickly be blown out of proportion due to flooding. The stress emotion doesn't turn off in their brain, telling them that there is a bear next to them when, in reality, it might be a hard homework problem.

Destressing can come in the form of CBT techniques such as running around outside, switching to a different assignment, or taking a break altogether, depending on how strong the reaction is.

Low Self-Esteem

Low self-esteem is not only caused by having ADHD. Society's reaction to the symptoms of ADHD also plays a significant role here.

Storytime! Nia is just entering the sixth grade and going to middle school for the first time. During her last couple of elementary school years, Nia was inside and learning because of the COVID-19 pandemic. She and her parents were able to develop strategies that helped her manage in the face of her ADHD. Thanks to working in an environment that was meeting her needs and a significant amount of hard work, Nia was at the top of her fifth-grade class.

Once she got into sixth grade, things became much more difficult. Her teachers had large class sizes and could not tend to her individually. She was expected to sit for six hours a day with little to no break. Her teachers often forgot that she had a 504 plan and would try to make her understand the same way as other students without trying another tactic. As one might expect, Nia's grades started slipping. Her heart dropped when she got her report card and saw that she had only made 'C's.' She was trying. Why were these grades there? Was she not doing it well enough? Was she not good enough?

In comes the problem of low self-esteem due to something that isn't her fault but the fault of a combination of things (ADHD, stifling environment, etc.).

This is a trap that many children with any setback can get into, and the flooding issue isn't going to make this any easier.

Self-esteem work is essential to anyone, especially in children with ADHD, and it can act to bring them back up after takedowns like the one above happen.

In Nia's case, self-esteem work might look like reminders. Some of the world's most brilliant minds are suspected of having ADHD, and look where they got us. We know that Nia can do it in the right environment, so maybe a switch needs to happen.

Finally, a 'C' is still a passing grade in Nia's case. It may be something to be improved on, but it is enough, which is what matters.

Procrastination

Procrastination is a problem for many of us, but for someone with ADHD, it can be even worse.

Let's say you are faced with a big project, and it is due in a month. You know that there is a lot to do, but you have enough time to do it by accomplishing little each day. Inside your brain, serotonin, our motivation chemical, is being released, and you have what you need to get started.

In someone with ADHD, serotonin is believed to be inhibited. Very little will come when the deadline is a month away. As the deadline gets closer and closer, a little bit more serotonin is released, but not enough for a person to get started. Eventually, the deadline for this massive project gets to be about a week away. There is finally enough serotonin. In fact, a person with ADHD may even experience flooding at this stage. The project still gets done, done well, and turned in on time, but to the rest of the people observing, the person with ADHD looks like they procrastinated.

The example above worked out, but remember, it does not always turn out like that. There is always a chance that the work will not get done on time, something significant will be missed, or the work turned in isn't the best.

Some ways people get around this include using extrinsic motivation (For example: if I finish section X of this report, I will have a good steak dinner tonight.), setting goals and using accountability partners, or pretending that the deadline is earlier than it actually is.

Why Do These Things Happen?

We have talked a lot about how the believed chemical makeup of the ADHD brain contributes to these issues. First of all, many of these things are consistent with an underdeveloped frontal lobe. The frontal lobe is responsible for many things, including things like emotional control, anger management, language, logic, and more. What we expect one kid to grasp may be unattainable to someone with ADHD.

The motivation chemical's lack of serotonin tells us why a child might procrastinate until the last second or why they might not pay attention. It's worth noting the things that are done on impulse that create an adrenaline rush also creates a rush of serotonin, so they are, in a way, motivated to commit thrill-seeking behaviors.

Flooding and a lack of incoming signals can be huge problems. I did include some simple tips for managing these issues, but ADHD is a lifelong condition, and longer-term solutions are often required.

Management Techniques

Okay, so your kiddo has ADHD. This issue comes with an inevitable question: now what? What happens now that you have a diagnosis? There are a lot of semi-long-term solutions and methods that have pros and cons, which we will be going into detail about below.

Medication

Medication is a popular treatment. As the amount of drugs created to treat these conditions increases, so does our prescription of them. Depending on the type of ADHD your child has and how it affects them, you might be prescribed a stimulant or non-stimulant medication. These will act on the issues in the brain and help bridge those gaps.

What are the pros of medication? It can work to make life easier for your child! In many cases, medication has largely solved the issue, and children go on to lead happy lives without the struggle of ADHD so long as they continue to take their meds.

That being said, this isn't the case for everyone. Medication will not work for every brain out there. Furthermore, it's not a one-size-fits-all situation. You may go through a couple of different prescriptions before finding the right one for your child.

Medications also have side effects. They are working in the brain and messing with brain chemicals, which could put a child at risk for mental health issues. The brain also adjusts to having these drugs, so if a child goes off of them after a long period, the symptoms might be worse. Finally, although rare, medication can affect the personality of an individual.

These side effects are things to consider when seeking treatment for your kiddo. They may or may not happen. At the end of the day, the choice of medication is up to you, your kiddo, and your doctor's recommendation.

Cognitive Behavioral Therapy

CBT studies the link between our thoughts, behaviors, and emotions. It recognizes that our emotions are the thing we have the least control over. Instead, they go with the flow of our thoughts and experiences. That being said, we have some control over our thoughts and, generally, a lot of control over our behavior. CBT techniques help you focus on your thoughts and emotions to lead to better outcomes.

For example, let's say that you're driving on the interstate when someone cuts across three lanes of traffic and right in front of you before suddenly slamming on their brakes. You do what's natural; you slam on your breaks, missing their car by inches. The people behind you also come to a dead stop as they try to avoid colliding with both of you and the other vehicles he cut off. Suddenly, he floors it and takes off at a pace way above the speed limit as if he did not nearly cause over a dozen cars to wreck into each other.

What's your initial emotion here? Most people would be understandably pretty upset. Your initial impulse might be to chase him down in a fit of road rage and either honk at him like a maniac or even cause him to crash. At the end of the day, though, what would that accomplish? At the very least, you're going to be held responsible.

Emotions that arise from situations like these can be especially troubling if you have a mental health condition or experience things like flooding. This is where CBT comes in. As you slowly start to move your car again, you notice how you feel, what thoughts you are having, and what behaviors you are experiencing. Then you implement strategies to help with any maladaptive thoughts or behaviors. This might come in handy for children when they are getting angry with someone or getting frustrated in a situation.

There are many techniques out there that your child might benefit from. A counselor or therapist can help direct you in choosing which ones are the best for your kiddo.

Coaching

ADHD impacts our ability to *do* things. Focusing on school, doing homework, household chores, and sometimes even basic self-care tasks can all get neglected in the face of ADHD. Coaching can help in one or more of these aspects. There is plenty that you can do yourself in this arena, but there are professionals who can also help.

A coach looking at self-care and other aspects of life might implement a routine that ensures that they can take care of themselves. They will also work on how to stick to this routine.

Someone may help with the cleaning by assisting them in devising a schedule that they can stick to and teaching them how to master it.

A tutor or a student aide can work with them on strategies for paying attention and being less disruptive in class on the school front. One approach has been to allow a child a fidget toy to focus their extra energy on while in school.

These are all roles that can be filled by you as well!

Talking Through Intensity

There may be things that seem to trigger intense, upsetting emotions for some children. You, and they, might not quite realize what this trigger is, but when they come across it, it leads to a full-blown meltdown.

First of all, help them calm down. No amount of talking is likely to get to them at this moment.

Once you are there, sit down with your kiddo. Ask them to walk you through what made them upset.

This walkthrough process will allow you to make the child aware that some behaviors they displayed were not okay. Since you are not in your child's mind and may not initially realize what went on there, it can also help you connect point 'A' to point 'B.' Finally, as stated above, it can help you identify what might be triggering an outburst. With that knowledge, you can work with your child on coping strategies for these triggers. Or, depending on the severity of the fit, you can help your kiddo avoid them altogether.

Some At-Home Tips

What things can you make a part of your child's routine to help them with everyday management?

Exercise

Children with ADHD seem to be full of boundless energy. Sitting still for long periods is already hard enough for them. Going straight to their study spaces might not be the best idea when they get home. They have already been sitting down for six to eight hours, and that energy has likely curled into a tight ball. Have a set time when they get home where they can get this energy out. If you can, try to encourage some exercise in the morning.

Martial Arts and Other Sports

Healthy activities add to the exercise factor for a kid. Sports involve a lot of running around and hard work, and they also add other benefits that regular exercise does not.

Martial arts, for example, gives them a chance to interact with their peers and a chance to release the frustration that they might have from the day.

Work With Words

Emotions can be shown and felt, but it's hard to understand them without knowing what's happening. One way to help your child with this is to give them the proper language to say how they are feeling, and this gives them a chance to talk through their emotions instead of blowing up.

Clear Boundaries and Rules

Have clear boundaries and rules in place the moment you can. Expectations and boundaries are things that the ADHD brain is good at molding. It also lets your child know what to expect when they come home. When they act out, it is a reference point that is very clear to your child.

Managing With New School Challenges

In late December of 2019, we learned about something that would change the world as we know it for the foreseeable future. Personally, at the time, I didn't realize that COVID-19 was going to be a big deal until about March when things started to look like they were going to shut down. It seemed that we were going about our lives as normal one day, and the next, we were getting prepared to homeschool our children. How did your kid manage with that adjustment?

Many struggled, and for ADHD children, there had to be many maddening aspects. Their routine was disrupted, and there was fear of going outside. Furthermore, all of that was on top of now having to attend school online. Even now, as exposures happen, children must be able to switch and continue their work without a teacher suddenly. How can you help your child with online learning as the world still goes through trouble spots?

What We Can Do

Plan a Schedule

You can let them know what you will be doing next by making a schedule. This schedule helps them have a sense of routine, even if something is going on right now.

Have Breaks

In your schedule, make sure that adequate break time is covered. Let them run around. Maybe try a youtube video or activity, and give them a chance to get up and move.

Timers and Clocks

Along with a written schedule that they can see, having a clock in their line of vision is an excellent step in ensuring that they know what is coming next. Timers can also help by giving them an audible notification of the start or end of a break.

Rewards

Do you ever have those days where you don't want to be productive no matter what is going on? This can feel even worse for someone with ADHD. When other strategies fail, it's okay to let them know those bad days are fine, but we still have to work through them. Extrinsic motivation in the form of rewards (A piece of candy for every page of an essay or 5 five minutes of screen time per lesson or assignment.) can help with these days!

Offer Support

The final part of both this struggle and the struggle of an ADHD child, in general, is to let them know that you are there to help. Offer your support as it's needed. It will help quite a bit in terms of your child's success.

Chapter Three
ADHD and Emotion Control

The first thing Mackenzie's mother notices is that she has woken up in what appears to be a nasty mood. She knows that it's just ADHD, but she can't help the dread about the potential fight she is about to face.

Mackenzie's mood seems to get worse as time goes on. She goes from appearing grouchy to now being snappy. From snappy, Mackenzie grows to become hostile. When her mom sits her down to do schoolwork, it happens. Mackenzie. Just. Blows. Up. The fit of screaming has Mackenzie red in the face. Both Mackenzie and her mom are shedding tears. She tries to reason with her, but Mackenzie has none of it. It takes about an hour before the outburst seems to be coming to an end. But, the end means that Mackenzie is still sobbing and feeling drained and miserable (After all, blowing up hasn't solved the issue and may have even made it worse.). She isn't stopping because she's no longer frustrated but rather because she doesn't have the energy to continue.

Mackenzie's mother is also feeling several after-effects, including stress, defeat, and some anger of her own. While she understands the concept of flooding, she has no idea what could have sent Mackenzie off in the first place.

This situation can be a reality for many people, and this chapter is designed to help you through it!

The Immediate Steps

We can try everything we know, but the occasional outburst is bound to happen, especially as young children, whether they have ADHD or not, don't yet have a full grasp of their emotions and how to handle them. Some things can be done to help manage and decrease episodes in the long run, but if you're in the position of Mackenzie's mother, what do you do while it's happening? And right afterward?

Time Them and Know

One of the most complex parts of this is that it can feel like an outburst that goes on for hours. You might end up left there feeling frustrated for a while before your kiddo finally calms down.

Start timing their meltdowns and get an idea of how long they last. This is strictly for you, and it gives you something to look at, and as you get an idea of what this looks like, it gives you a general idea of when this will end.

Keep Track Of Strategies That Work

You've probably already tried quite a few strategies for helping them. Some will have worked, and some will have not. That is okay. However, either write down or mentally keep track of the ones that did help. Hold onto these for later use! You never know when you might need it!

Save The Talking for Later

At the moment, your words aren't going to reach them. After Mackenzie finally stopped and sat on the floor crying, She wasn't even aware that her mother had said anything to her during those moments. Many children end up in the same position.

Worse, if those words are said in anger or with an angry tone, children will jump on this and use it as fuel for the fire. Save your words for later, when your kiddo is able to comprehend them. It will help you a lot in the long run!

Get Everyone Calm

When we left Mackenzie, she was still crying. While this might seem like everything is over, in Mackenzie's brain, it isn't. There are still things going on that we aren't quite aware of. Furthermore, Mackenzie's mom is likely to be wound up over this.

Give your kiddo a chance to stop crying and calm down. While they do that, this is the perfect moment for you to calm down and take a few deep breaths.

Help With Emotion Identification

Finally, once everyone is calm, we can start tackling what caused this in the first place. Why did World War Three just happen in your home?

Younger children especially may not yet know what sets them off, just that something did. Walk them through what just happened. Ask them about their emotions in those moments. If they don't know the words, have them describe them to you and see if you can help give them words to use.

Now, first of all, they know the emotions that they are feeling during this process. Second, they've had a chance to walk through what happened. You might be able to figure out what triggered the outburst, and they have a chance to see that their actions weren't the right ones to take.

Discipline In the Face of a Meltdown

Is it your kiddo's fault that their brain isn't wired as well for stressful situations? No. Are they still responsible for their actions? Yes. Is the outside world going to let them blow up whenever they want? No.

Discipline is the way to allow this gap to fill. I want to note that we are talking about directing, learning opportunities, and experiencing consequences that directly relate to their actions. This does not refer to punishment, which is often a physical or psychological thing that does not relate to the issue. Punishment on any child, but especially in children with ADHD, is highly ineffective. Discipline, like the methods below, aims to help teach.

Public Situations

Mackenzie's meltdown took place in the privacy of her own home. That doesn't always happen, especially when you consider that public spaces often have a lot of stimuli that can be overwhelming to a person with ADHD or any disability that involves brain function. A public meltdown can be the absolute worst, but there are effective ways to work through it.

First of all, if you know that your child is likely overwhelmed in a public space, sit down and talk about what it feels like. Help them understand some of the things that happen when they start to get overwhelmed. Let them know that it's okay to come to you and tell you that they need a break. Or, as they get older, let them know it's okay for them to take a break.

If you start noticing signs of a meltdown, try to separate them from the public atmosphere as quickly as possible. Stop the downturn before it happens, if it's possible. If not, pull your child to a safe space, like your car.

Always treat leaving as an option. If your child is having a lot of trouble calming down, it may be best to leave and return to an environment where your child is comfortable. After a meltdown happens, your child will still be feeling many upsetting emotions, and they are also likely to be drained. Going home lets everyone calm down, and it also acts as a form of a natural consequence. It's okay to feel how you're feeling, but it's best to separate from the situation if things become too much.

Avoid Obvious Anger

In the moment of a meltdown, your child will not hear words. If they do catch what you're saying and perceive it to be angry, you might have an even worse problem on your hands.

Anger is something that the ADHD brain treats like a fuse. Once that fuse is lit, there aren't many things that can stop that bomb from going off.

If you can feel your anger start to build up, don't engage. Take a minute to calm yourself down first! Then, try to speak with your kiddo peacefully. Remaining calm, even if they try to escalate the situation, is often the best way to ensure that things are handled in a way that helps a lesson be learned!

Separate

Whether they realize it or not, one standard method used by many parents is to separate the child from the environment. This is essentially a time-out, and while it's mainly used for toddlers, it's great for everyone (including adults).

A time-out will, first of all, separate them from the situation. Your child has had a meltdown or done something they shouldn't have, and it is time to step away.

Next, it gives everyone a chance to calm down. They are upset, and you are upset. A time-out is needed to give everyone a break and a chance to breathe.

Finally, it gives them a chance to reflect on what has just happened.

Once everyone has had their chance to calm down, talking through the circumstance will be received. This includes having them explain their thought process and letting them know that certain behaviors are not okay.

As human beings, we are all prone to and allowed to have our emotions. It's okay for you to be angry, upset, and frustrated.

In these moments, it can be tempting to yell and use punishment methods to deal with the behavior, especially since punishment often has an effect known as instant obedience. In the long run and sometimes in the short run, things will only worsen. It can destroy communication that you have worked hard to build. It can cause your child to try to contain their emotions, which will lead to an explosion later.

Talking through it is much more effective because it gives you and the kiddo a chance to learn and set the boundaries that the behavior isn't acceptable.

Stick To Your Guns

Children with ADHD have brains that do not naturally structure themselves, and they have to rely on their environment to provide this structure for them.

This is another reason why punishment can be a bad idea. Kids with ADHD don't know what to expect next. Instead, having rules in place can make a difference.

It's important to note that your kiddo is likely to resist if you are starting with new strategies. For example, if you, in the past, relied on spanking, and you are now asking your child to walk through what happened and potentially admit where they went wrong, then there is a good chance that they will resist by not staying in time out, or refusing to walk through anything. It can sometimes take several weeks or even a couple of months to solidify in place. When they resist, don't go back to the old method. Tempting as it may be, you left it because it was not helping.

That being said, hold your expectations clear. Every time they get up from a time out or a cool down, set them back down and restart the timer. When they refuse to explain, sit there for as long as is needed.

Strategies For Emotional Balance Through the Day

We would all like to prevent a meltdown or outburst before it happens. Think back to Mackenzie. There were warning signs that she might blow up from the start, and her mom was dreading it. The good news is that deregulation can begin right here, and it doesn't have to wait until someone hits the nuclear button. Some of these strategies are in the moment, and others are things you can add to your everyday routine to bring about a more central sense of peace.

Describing Feelings

Relating emotions gets a mention here as it is so important. We can't control how we feel during the day, only how we react to the things around us. Knowing how we feel and putting that into words plays a considerable part in our ability to control how we act. Start teaching these things to your child. There are many books for kids that focus on learning emotions through stories. After meltdowns, there are also opportunities to give them new words to describe how they feel.

If you notice that your child's day starts similarly to how Mackenzie's did, or you notice a change in mood at any point, pull them aside and ask them to check in and describe what they are feeling. Deregulation and a plan not to let those feelings ruin any fun will be immensely beneficial.

Having A Long-Term Plan

Children with ADHD cannot process anger the same way we do and often find that it floods their emotional response abilities. Furthermore, ADHD does correlate with emotional and anger management problems.

This can be an irregular struggle for many, especially if you have a child that blows up quite a lot. Along with this, your child may be becoming a teen who wants more independence but is still suffering from issues due to their ADHD. It may be time to make a long-term plan with your kiddo. The older they are, the more involved they can be.

The first step to most emotional plans is recognizing the emotions you are facing and accepting when it's time to step away! What stepping away might look like can be a part of the plan.

There also needs to be a way to enforce this. There might be a written contract between the parent and the child, and there might be some direct consequences due to an outburst or a behavior issue. Whatever the case is, it is laid out clearly for the child to help them improve.

Meditation

There are many great uses for meditation for a child with ADHD. Meditation is a practice of calm, and you are in a relatively quiet space and focusing on the stimulus you receive.

A typical mediation would involve you sitting down and closing your eyes. You would start breathing deeply and focusing just on that. Once you have confidently concentrated on your breathing, you might do a body scan. Using this, you can find and release tension that's stored in your muscles. Managing a sound and complete scan of your body, start expanding your focus outward. Pay attention to any breeze or AC you might be feeling on your skin. Focus on any smells or sounds around you. You can do this for as long as you like, and then you will slowly come back to your body and then to your breathing.

Meditation helps with things like mental clarity, and it has shown to be a great practice that anyone can benefit from. Of course, children with ADHD might struggle with this at first, and everyone does. Many beginners use music, guided meditations, or a combination of the two.

Guided meditations have an additional benefit because they often have little reminders for when your focus drifts away. You can find these on Spotify, Youtube, or any app based on meditation.

If your child needs some extra help, then try some games. Meditation-based games can act as distractors, and they can help you help your kiddo.

One game is specifically for breathing. Does your child have a favorite toy or stuffed animal? If so, use it for the game. Have your child lay down and place the object on their chest. Have them breathe deeply and watch the movement of the object. Once it seems that they are calm, have them describe it to you.

You can make meditation as a whole into a game by being their guide and using appropriate language for their age.

For example, "we sit straight and tall now" and "it's okay to feel squirmy, but I must sit still now."

Walking meditations are also great, but you will absolutely need to be there for this one, as they will close their eyes as they walk. Guide them through meditation as they are walking and help them be in tune with their senses.

Finally, there is a game of freezing in place. If your child is having a hyperactive moment, instruct them to freeze in place. Give them a moment of stillness before asking questions. Draw their attention inward if you can. Ask them about how their body is doing. Does it feel any different right now?

These practices help your kiddo learn to regulate and deal with their emotions in productive ways. Down the line, anyone can use these strategies no matter their age!

Being Gentle With Yourself

Many struggles come with raising a child with ADHD. Some days you will feel fantastic, and on a lot of days, you will sit down and wonder what you did to deserve this.

It's not worth it to bottle up your emotions. You are also a person, and you deserve love and support through the challenges that come your way.

It's normal to feel angry and frustrated, and it's normal to make mistakes. Wanting to yell at your kid when they are acting out is also normal, especially if that's how you were raised. However, knowing that it will make the situation worse makes the burden that much harder.

You have to be gentle with yourself. Just like your child is allowed to feel what they feel, you are too! Take a few pages for yourself. Work through your emotions and acknowledge them. If you need a break, take it. Do what you need to do to get yourself together. If it's several minutes later when you address the situation, that's okay.

Don't be afraid to take the time you need before moving into effective discipline strategies. Our next chapter will get into more depth on discipline and what to keep in mind even after the meltdown has happened.

Chapter Four
Good or Bad Disciplines?

Let us consider the history of discipline for a moment. Well, I'm using the term discipline lightly. Think back to your own experience as a child. Were you spanked? Were the adults angry at you in your life, and sometimes it seemed to be without reason?

These methods were founded on religious-based ideology (For example, "spare the rod, spoil the child."), and it was just the best information we had at the moment until a few decades ago.

Now, we see that this hurts the development of typical children, and in children with conditions like ADHD, it can be especially harmful because their brain isn't processing it in the same manner.

Spanking is a great example because so much research has come about. It harms children psychologically (increased rates of depression and anxiety), can contribute to anger management and violence issues, and interestingly enough, it doesn't work. Children who have been spanked are more likely to repeat the same behavior. While spanking leads to your child listening to you at that moment, a lesson isn't learned (As seen by them being statistically more likely to repeat what they just got in trouble for.).

If you have spanked your child in the past, it doesn't make you a bad parent, especially if you don't have this information.

So, what methods should you use with corporal punishment off the table? You want to relay that some behavior isn't acceptable, but how do you do this in a way that your child can understand? Science has told us that practices like spanking don't work, and it's also clued us into what might help.

Keep in mind a few things. First, every child is different. Your child may respond to some methods but not others, and that's okay. Second, if you are switching to a new approach, there is a good chance your child will resist. We talked about this a little bit in chapter three, but if you think about it, using spanking means your child endures it and then goes back to whatever they are doing. Sitting down to talk takes longer, and they have to participate, admit what they might have done wrong, and plan to fix it. That is not comfortable, especially at first. Plus, with methods like spanking, your child is more likely to be defiant in the long run. It might take a couple of months for the resistance to stop and for you to see fundamental changes. I promise that it will be worth it.

What To Do Before You Use a New Method

It will be essential for you, the parent, to start implementing some things even before you bring it to your child's attention that there will be some new things going on around them. Let's start here.

Your Role

As the parent, you are your child's role model and the person they look to when things aren't going quite right. When you are implementing a new method, it can be more stressful when a child has ADHD. Any inconsistency will be a triggering signal that will take ten times as long to undo as it did to create. Understandably, that might make you feel like you can't make a mistake. You're human, and we are allowed to make mistakes as humans. Still, you can get ready with some strategies to help with this complex issue.

First, work on self-discipline. Train your mind to be calm and patient in these meltdowns. Focus on carrying a sense of calm with you throughout the day, no matter what's happening.

If you feel that things are starting to get to you, it's okay to step out and take a break. Do what you need to do for yourself first. It will help you and your kiddo for you to do so.

Establish a Routine

We've talked about a routine before, and it's getting brought up again in a different light. What happens after a meltdown or a behavior issue? Have a procedure in place for this.

After a meltdown, it can include a cooling-off moment, followed by a talk, and if appropriate, a clearly laid out consequence.

If the conduct continues, behavior issue routines might look like a warning, followed by an initiated consequence.

Consistency like this leaves your child knowing what to expect when they have an outburst or break the rules. It creates a balance that everyone can count on.

Behaviors Outside Your Child's Control

It is very tempting to feel like we need to act on every wrongdoing for our kids to grow up successfully. This isn't the case at all! In fact, it can be damaging to do so.

ADHD comes with a range of behaviors that are genuinely outside your child's control. By reverting to discipline strategies, it can make them feel like a bad kid who can't control that they are "bad." This sense of a lack of control can lead to them stopping effort on good behavior.

The first thing to recognize is that your child makes mistakes and has bad days, much like you. No one in this world is perfect, which is a concept that many people struggle with. Children with ADHD may see being perfect as behaving in a way that makes it so that no one knows they have ADHD. This is unrealistic, as it may be perceived that not having ADHD means that you don't make mistakes. Self-esteem is a common struggle, and being there to reinforce that everyone makes mistakes can be a great buffer.

Another common issue you might run into that is out of your child's control is that of labeling. If you remember, back in chapter two, we talked about Nia. Nia had ADHD and was diagnosed shortly before the pandemic. The two years she spent doing school at home were incredible. They were able to cater to her needs and create a schedule that allowed her to function optimally. She was the highest performer in her fifth-grade class. Then, when she got to sixth grade, she ran into issues. The environment was no longer a strength for her, and at the end of the day, she only received 'C's,' which were passing but not what she was hoping for. As previously accomplished, Nia's capable of getting high marks when her needs are met. When they aren't, she is different.

Your child is very likely to run into similar things, and many teachers are quick to put the blame on the ADHD and add labels like "too slow" or "not likely to succeed." Don't listen to this. First of all, for a teacher to do that is entirely wrong. Second, it's rarely the child. Work with them. Find out what their challenges are. See if there are ways for their needs to be met.

It's important to remember that symptoms of ADHD are not the teacher's fault. Teachers have several children to attend to at any given time, and it can be difficult to pay attention to one kid. Don't assign blame to them or anyone else when the thing in the way is ADHD. When that's our focus, that is the problem we tackle.

Another thing is to distinguish which misbehavior is caused by intention and which are symptoms of ADHD. Imagine, for a moment, that you asked for your kid to help with laundry. They go and grab the laundry, but minutes later, you come out to find the laundry dumped all over the living room and your child staring at the window. This is caused by distraction, which is very common in someone with ADHD. Instead of moving to discipline, as they can't control this behavior, aim for redirection.

In this case, see what distracted your child, acknowledge that it is okay, and then remind them that they have a task to be doing.

A tip from experts is to avoid saying no when you can or to at least give an explanation when you do. When you say no often and with no explanation, any child will be upset. A child with ADHD is going to be impulsive. When you say no without reason, the no isn't enough. They will likely do it anyway and potentially get hurt.

Finally, modeling the behaviors you want to see can help. Your child is looking to you for guidance, and practicing the methods you want them to pick up will have its own effect.

Being a center of calm can help a lot when having ADHD. Modeling Behaviors that you would like to see can help too!

Different Strategies

How do you make discipline stick? What will help your child understand right and wrong without going as far as punishment?

Daily Uplifting Interactions

Imagine that you are a child, and your parents rarely interact with you, except when there is either a significant event or for discipline. You can certainly go for a few days with almost no interaction from this parent. But, what happens when you do something that you shouldn't?

As a child, when this is your relationship with either parent, would you say that you are much less likely to take what they say seriously? You may comply, but more out of fear of losing privileges rather than any understanding of what you did wrong.

Now think about having the opposite relationship with a parent. There is positive interaction every single day, and they make it a point to be involved in all the big and small things.

Children with a parent like this have every opportunity to make themselves seen and heard. Subsequently, children with this type of parent are much more likely to listen to them in the face of discipline.

Most parents exist on a spectrum between these two. Aiming for the latter, even if it is just for 15 minutes each day, can significantly impact the presence of behavioral problems and how discipline is taken.

Careful Direction

It is a busy morning, and as you make breakfast, your child comes over. After greeting them, you give them a few tasks.

"I need you to make your bed, get dressed, feed the cat, and take out the trash." Your child nods and skips off. You come up later to find the bed mostly made and your child half-dressed, wearing pants, a single sock, and still in their pyjama shirt. Their other sock is on their hand as a sock puppet. You don't know whether to laugh or get angry.

As amusing as sock puppets are, it's safe to say that the kiddo got distracted, which is common in people with ADHD.

You listed a few things at once, and they only made it halfway due to their ADHD. A good fix is to put these tasks on a list that they have for reference. This is something that lets them focus on one task at a time!

Pay Attention to the Good Behavior and Let Your Child Know

With children who have typically developing brains, using discipline with bad behavior and letting good behavior happen or simply saying "good job" can suffice.

Children with ADHD need much more reinforcement. When your child has a quality day after a string of bad ones, let them know you see it. When you notice that a task you constantly ask them to do has been completed that day without saying anything, let them know they did a good job and be specific with your words. The ADHD brain creates a feedback loop with positive reinforcement, so this will make them more likely to repeat these behaviors.

Consequences That Are a Result Of Their Actions

We learn a lot when our lack of planning, or something else that is our fault, gets in our way. With ADHD, this can be a strong motivator, and how a lesson ends up sticking. For example, let's say your child refuses to put their coat on in the morning. Let them try going to school without it. When they are inevitably cold, they will remember when it is time to put on their coat the next day.

Using these can help your strategies stick in the long run. Next are just a few extra tips to help round up the chapter!

Extra Tips

These tips come from people who have experience working with kids who have ADHD. Here are some of their recommendations.

Do vs. Don't

We have all seen the typical house rules that use words like "no" and "don't." For an ordinary child, this works okay, but for someone with ADHD, these might be natural impulses and are likely to think, "well, now what?" Instead, make lists of rules that contain "do" statements. Instead of "no running," change it to "walk when you're inside." Instead of "no fighting," change it to "everyone will play nicely together."

Keep a Tally of Behavior

Children with ADHD need things that they can see in order to be able to remember them. An excellent method to help with behavior is to have a reward system in place. Each time a child completes the desired behavior, add something to the chart. You can assign rewards differently (Ex. draw your reward, random rewards, rewards that increase in size the more points they get, etc.).

Keep It Visible

Visibility can apply to many things, including rules, rewards, chores, and a daily routine. Have something visible so that everyone can know what's going on, especially your kiddo!

Show What You Are Asking

Going back to visibility. If you are trying to teach your child new chores or other things, don't just tell them what to do. Your child isn't likely to learn it. Instead, show them.

Walkthrough the task and show them what to do each step of the way. When it's your child's turn, let them show you what to do so you can make sure they have the hang of it!

Have A Safe, Cool Down Space

Offering a cool-down space can be for during or after a meltdown or if your child notices that they are starting to get into one and want to calm themselves.

This space should be as separate from the rest of the house as possible. There shouldn't be too much going on in the area in terms of the senses. Put a chair or beanbag and possibly a stuffed toy in this area and make it known that they can come there if they aren't having a good day.

These strategies and tips can go a long way in helping you bring peace to your home, but it's not all about discipline. There are some other things that are highly important to do with ADHD children!

Chapter Five
Burn That Energy With Activities

A huge part of having ADHD seems to be that a ton of energy floods in with the diagnosis. There is a lot to keep track of as your little one seems to bounce off the walls. ADHD is not about sitting still, to say the least. What do you do instead?

All of these activities below are designed to burn energy. There are some indoor and some outdoor options so that no matter what the weather is, you have some tricks up your sleeve.

Dance Parties

Partying down with some dance moves can be great for indoor and outdoor time. You can plan these or have them at any moment that you feel that you need to. Music is very accessible with many of the devices we have today, and if you can get the volume loud enough, you don't even need a speaker. You can have your dance party be an hour-long or a break for one song when you notice your child's concentration on homework dropping.

A Scavenger Hunt

Again, a scavenger hunt can be great outside, but this can also be perfect if you're stuck inside on a rainy day. You can hide anything you want, and this might include stuffed animals, small-dollar tree items, random silverware, leftover easter eggs, or anything else that you have a lot of lying around. The more complicated you make this activity, the more fun they will have with it and the more energy they will burn.

Create A Course With Common Items

Again, a good obstacle course has indoor and outdoor wonders to it. Everyday items such as boxes and cardboard can become anything with little imagination. A giant box can be a car, a boat, a battleship, or whatever you deem fit to make into a game. You can make a lot of cardboard into a maze or a tiny house. Building a fort out of cardboard, pillows, blankets, and more can make this a fun activity that takes energy and makes a great place to quietly spend time when the energy is gone.

Painters tape is something else that you can use, and it won't create any damage. You can use this to create courses (making them follow the line) or build simple boards to use in games like hopscotch or four square. The possibilities with simple items can be endless if we put our minds to them.

Get a Balance Board

Inside and outside are great places to use a balance board. Children with ADHD may lack coordination and other gross motor skills, which can help. A simple balance board will keep them relatively still while expending a ton of energy. This shouldn't come with much of an injury hazard, but if your child is a fan of quick and sudden movements, try to avoid doing this on hard surfaces (like concrete, for example)!

Playing Ball... With Balloons

This is especially helpful for inside days. Balloons can be made for just about any game, including dodgeball, tennis, volleyball, baseball, and even a game of catch. The perfect thing about this is that most of these options are inside-friendly when using a balloon!

Inside Friendly Toys That You Don't Normally Think About

There are certainly some outside toys that should remain outside and some that are rather versatile.

Hula hoops can be used inside so long as there isn't anything breakable nearby. Another example is a jump rope, and both can take up a lot of time as an activity, expand energy, and be perfectly safe inside.

A final example is an exercise ball. This can be used to play on, but if you notice that it's harder for your kiddo to stay during homework or mealtime, switch them to an exercise ball so that they can bounce away and focus better. If you're worried about them falling, exercise ball chairs lock the ball in place and have wheels so you can still move the chair, but there is much less fall risk.

Group Activities

Socialization is important for everyone, and group activities provide the option for everyone to be included. Children with ADHD will especially have a hard time picking up social cues. Activities with friends can be a great way to bridge the gap. You can try sports like soccer, baseball, dance, football, etc. You can also look into active workshops, like swim lessons and day camps during school off times. All of these give your kiddo a chance to get out of the house (which gives you a chance to rest) and make new friends while getting into something they might enjoy.

Solo Sports

Social cue understanding is not the only thing that gets delayed in children due to ADHD. Another thing that I mentioned above was gross motor skills.

Gross motor skills deal with big movements like running, jumping, hand-eye coordination, and balance. Fine motor skills, its counterpart, deal with things like writing, art, and smaller overall movements.

With their gross motor skills falling behind, your kiddo may be more prone to injury from a fall. They might have a reputation for being a little clumsy. In the long run, it's essential to look at some solo activities to help this. And in addition to working on your motor skills, your kiddo will run off a lot of energy. Biking is a great way to do this. So is swimming. A trip to the park that gives them a chance to play on equipment can help too!

Trampoline

Okay, pretty much everyone out there would look at a trampoline and say "yes." They are fun, and you can spend hours jumping away if you wish, and this very springy material is constantly thwarting gravity's effect. You can have games on here or constantly bounce, and the choice is up to you and your kiddo.

On a side note, there are also smaller indoor trampolines that are especially enjoyed by toddlers and young children, which can also provide hours of entertainment.

Knock Out Some Chores

How fun getting some chores done depends on how creative you can get. Outdoor chores, in particular, can be a great way to burn energy.

Gardening can be a great example, especially if your kiddo has a particular interest in the outdoors, plants, or science.

Another example is car washing. Not only is something getting done, but there is lots of fun to be had. And let's be honest, no one is walking away without being completely soaked.

Water Fight

Summer and warm days come around once a year for everyone. During these times, it's nice to cool off somehow, and an impromptu water fight is an excellent way for you, your kiddo, and potentially a few other people, to do so. Get water guns and water balloons, and get whatever you can to make this a fun adventure! Is everyone going to be soaking wet after this? Yes! Will it be worth it? Yes! Everyone involved will have expended a lot of energy!

Yoga

Yoga is excellent for the body, as it gives us a chance to stretch and feel muscles that we might not have entirely realized were there before. Getting your kiddo a yoga mat and some kid-friendly Youtube videos can help them get started with this.

Let it Fly

Don't worry. I'm only talking about paper airplanes. It may seem like such a simple thing as adults, but we all seemed to get so much joy out of making a paper airplane as children. Introduce this idea to your kiddo and watch things fly!

Sculptures

There are so many different ideas when it comes to sculpting!

This engages your child's fine motor skills, creativity, and thought process. The medium is up to you. You can use playdough, modeling clay, kinetic sand, Lego, or whatever else you can find to build with.

Art

Drawing and coloring take energy and are very therapeutic, which is true for painting as well! There are many things here that aren't messy (or are at least easy to clean) that can occupy your kiddo for hours and work on their energy levels.

Take Advantage of Things In Your Community

The biggest example of things to do in your community is attending the library. Go out in public and expend a lot of energy. A library is a great place to go, especially for young kids, because many things in your area can be found there. They often also have kids' groups where your child can take part. Libraries are public but also quiet, so your kiddo is less likely to find themselves overwhelmed.

Other places include parks, community centers, the local YMCA, and more! A quick search can tell you what is nearby.

Concentration Based Activities

Our brains take up a lot of our energy each day. When you work, even if it's a desk job, you probably find yourself tired at the end of the day as you have used a significant portion of your brain.

Children with ADHD often have a hard time sitting still and doing something unless it is of interest. These games are designed to keep them interested, help them develop their brain, and burn a little bit of the excess brain energy we all have.

Sequencing and Matching Games

There are a few options for sequencing and matching games. Memory cards are a simple choice. They can help your kiddo match things, and it also helps with memory. When you turn over a card you have seen before, you must remember where you saw it last. While children with ADHD struggle with memory, games like this can help the brain bridge the gap. There are other, more complex, sequencing board games that kiddos can try as their ability to handle specific difficulties increases.

If you want to increase the difficulty, find a few small objects. Coins or dice are some great examples. Once you have these items, find a piece of cardboard.

Now for the game. Give yourself and your kiddo some of these objects and arrange yours in a row.

For example, if you are using dice, you might put five of them in a row and have them say something like "three, five, four, two, one." Give your kiddo a second to look at it, and then cover the dice with your paper. Have your kiddo make the same pattern and then lift your sheet. If they remembered correctly, congratulate them, and give them a new sequence. Whether you increase the difficulty or not is up to you. If they do not get it right, give them a chance to look it over again before replacing the block and have them try again.

Games such as these are active and one-on-one, so it will be harder for your kiddo to get distracted. They will also serve your kiddo well in the long run by building strength in their memory.

Simon Says

You can get just about everyone involved in some Simon Says. Great for memory, it can be perfect for one's attention span. The child must pay attention to each word to play the game properly. Again, this can help the brain make even more connections.

Puzzles

Puzzles are perfect for teaching problem-solving skills. In order to put together a puzzle, a child has to fit several tiny images together to make a picture. It is not going to get done unless they work on it, so kids are likely to gravitate toward getting it done.

You do not have to make use of jigsaw puzzles to do this. Crosswords, word searches, sudoku, and online platforms can all contain similar challenges that keep your kiddo occupied and using energy for quite some time.

Active Video Games

Things like the Wii or Kinect for Xbox involve body movements in the quest to play games. There are dancing games, sports games, and more! Obviously, these aren't cheap! Many people who play these games post them on Youtube. While it won't keep a score, you can use these videos for motions for your kiddo to mimic. Children of all ages and abilities are often able to occupy themselves for hours using this!

Older Kids

Let's face it; children grow up. There are many activities listed above that an older kiddo in their teen years might reject because they feel like it is for young children. Up next is our list of activities specifically for teens. Here we're going to talk about some new methods and build on the ones we have already discussed.

Martial Arts

Martial art forms may serve teens even more than they benefit children.

ADHD creates loose connections in the brain that can't always handle hormones and chemicals that are there for brain health. Going through puberty floods the system with these very same hormones and chemicals. Martial arts can be aggressive. You can fight in martial arts, and you learn defense. You also literally get to break boards in martial arts using only your strength.

There is an additional benefit that applies more to teens. As your child grows, they are going to want to spend more time outside of the house, by themselves, and with friends. People with ADHD aren't always as aware of their surroundings as others, which can make them an easy target. If your teen has self-defense skills at the ready, you can be assured that they are going to be okay and can protect themself.

Scavenger Hunt: Teen Addition

As a teenager, an in-home scavenger hunt is probably just looking for where they misplaced their phone. However, they might have some fun with them, but not as much as a little one. Luckily, you can make the same concept just a little bigger. Have you ever heard of geocaching? What about letterboxing? Geocaches are hidden in places worldwide, and likely some are very close to you. These might be little pill bottles or whole boxes filled with goodies that you can swap out. There are entire communities dedicated to geocaching.

Much of the same is true with letterboxing. This is very similar to geocaching, but the concept is different. You will need a simple notebook and possibly an ink pad for letterboxing. A letterbox is hidden similarly to a geocache, but inside will be one thing: a stamp and an ink pad (Sometimes these might be dried out, so it can be handy to have your own with you.). These stamps can be letters, numbers, characters, or just something else that happens to be really cool!

Activities like this can be done alone if your teen would like some time to themself, and they can also be done with friends and as a family. At the end of the day, you will have burnt a lot of energy, which can be an excellent source of fun!

Sports

As kids enter middle and high school, sports become more prominent. There are multiple reasons to get your kiddo involved in sports at the high school age. It has similar benefits for children, but you need to maintain specific grades in high school to stay in sports. This can be hugely incentivizing if your kid has a sport they enjoy.

Building On Art

As a child turns into a teenager, the art your kiddo will likely want to do is going to grow. Painting and drawing may become more complicated, as will other art forms. Let them experiment. It takes a fair bit of energy, and it's building neural connections.

You might try some adult-based coloring books and adult paint by number sheets to foster this. From there, let your teens' creativity come to life.

Making Music

Your child might like singing or marching band or even be in their own small band. Encourage these things; there are many reasons why you should. For starters, music has had reparative effects on many brains. In the case of ADHD, it could foster some amazing developmental steps. It's also another fun way to let out some creativity.

Theater

The art form of the theater still exists in many schools, and where there aren't schools, there are usually other programs. Teens who enjoy being creative can find many things in the theater.

There is, of course, the actual performance side. But, there is also set and costume design, directing, controlling the stage, lighting, singing, and more. In short, there is something in theater for everyone.

Board Games

Our final recommendation is board games (of course). These have been around forever, and they encourage some great things.

The older your kiddo is, the more advanced these games can get. The game of Life, Monopoly, and others can be great for fun and challenging loving teens. You can even look at story-based games. An example of a hardcore story game would be Dungeons & Dragons.

There are many different activities that your child can get invested in to help keep their ADHD at a manageable level. These give a wide range of ideas for all ages to participate. Your child might not love some of them, but they may come to really enjoy others. As we discussed in a previous chapter, take a second to find what works. Then, give that a solid go.

Chapter Six

Nutrition and Well-Being

If you recall, there was a teeny paragraph about health and nutrition several chapters ago. That paragraph does not do justice to the issue. Diet is of vital importance to everyone. In America especially, the laws on what preservatives and additives can be added to food are pretty lax. So long as it will not immediately poison a person, you can pretty much get away with it. Because of this, we have to be especially careful of what we are adding.

Let's visit two children in the fifth grade. Both have ADHD-combined types.

Esme gets up and has eggs and berries for breakfast. Her mother packs her lunch and sends her to school.

Cameron wakes up and eats some toaster waffles for breakfast. His mother has also packed his lunch before he goes to school.

Both Esme and Cameron sit in class. While Esme is constantly fidgeting with a little cube that she has on her desk, at the very least, she seems to be paying attention and getting her work done.

On the other hand, Cameron is bouncing up and down in his seat. He keeps staring at windows, other students, and anywhere else that isn't the whiteboard he is supposed to be looking at. It bugs his teacher to no end, but she tries to be patient, knowing that it isn't his fault.

Both children eat lunch. Amy's lunch contains some leftover whole wheat pasta from the other night and some chicken and vegetables. She gets a Gatorade as well, and Cameron takes a Lunchable as well as an apple and a juice box.

During recess, both kids are running around like crazy. After all, they have been sitting inside all day. However, as they line up to go back inside, Esme seems worn out but alert. On the other hand, Cameron has an exhausted look on his face. He keeps trying not to fall asleep in class, and he crashes about an hour later. The teacher wakes him up but lets it go when he falls asleep a second time. Both are picked up, and as they go home, both have the same energy levels again.

Despite the same diagnosis, you can see how they behaved differently throughout the day. This is a common pattern with everyone. Let's take a look a little further into this.

The Why and the How

Why did Cameron seem so different? To be honest, when a typical child is given a lot of processed foods in a day, they will struggle. Again, it's challenging to do something about this in some countries because preservatives seem to be in everything. I promise though that it is worth the effort. Some foods seem to positively impact brainpower, leading us to believe that they can help with ADHD.

This does beg the question, "how do I get my child to eat it?"

Cameron's mom knows that he is a picky eater. Along with this, she has to consider the fact that she works, so she cannot make a meal from scratch every day. Many moms and dads are in the same position, and I feel you on this!

One way to help your child has to do with the power of natural consequences. Remember a few chapters ago, we looked at a little one who didn't want to put their coat on. Rather than battling them about it, the parents let them go without it. The child did find herself cold throughout the day and learned the importance of wearing her coat. A similar effect can be taught with the food that we consume.

When your child refuses to consume food that is better for them, in favor of consuming highly processed food, let it happen at least for a full day. When their energy levels deplete and they have a more challenging time with day-to-day tasks, help them connect to the fact that the food causes this. When they have a better diet day, mention how great it is that they can focus so well and that it must be because they ate so well. Making this distinction will help your child naturally understand how their diet influences their energy levels.

Meal prep is another thing that parents can do for themselves if they find that they are swamped throughout the week (as many of us are). This doesn't have to be super complicated. You can make a giant batch of a single meal or a few medium-sized batches of meals that everyone likes and pull from that through the week. Alternatively, divide it into containers right at the beginning; the choice is yours.

For kids that absolutely refuse and are generally picky eaters, you can knock many healthy things back into them by making them yourself. You can make homemade pizzas, chicken tenders, and other common foods at home with ingredients you can find pretty much anywhere. It also gives you an idea of what your kiddo is actually consuming.

Finally, involve your kiddos in the process, especially if they are older. If your child is a teen, you can have them choose the ingredients at the store and make their lunch, with help as needed. For younger kiddos, they can also assist in making lunches and helping you prepare some of the meals listed above.

Many kids, especially those whose brains are wired a bit differently, prefer foods that taste good and are familiar, and this especially pertains to junk foods. It often takes several different strategies to teach kids about foods that are generally better for them. It's absolutely worth it, though!

MyPlate

Let's start with this question: what does healthy food look like? Today, diet culture sends messages about good and bad foods and tells you what you should eat. Many diet plans out there focus on telling you exactly what to eat and eliminating certain food groups, which will not help you and will not help your kiddo.

The vast majority of certified people in diet and health sciences all refer back to one thing: MyPlate. MyPlate is the American government's research diet system. It does not eliminate anything, but it focuses on what foods are better for you and what you should put more focus on eating. MyPlate isn't the only existing database like this. Many countries have their own versions based on a healthy diet and take into account the food produced in that area.

If you're looking for some information specific to your kiddo, you might find some help through the MyPlate website or the website specific to your region.

Foods To Focus On

Your child's diet does not have to contain healthy foods solely, but as you create meals for your little ones, these are the best things to have the most focus on.

Complex Carbs

Here is the first one! Now, many diet programs say that carbs are a terrible food and you should cut them out; don't do that! Carbohydrates are what our bodies thrive on, and while some carbs are a sugar load, others are not. As you might imagine, complex carbs fall into the latter category.

Carbs (both complex carbs and simple carbs) are energy units. How much energy something will give you is determined by how many carbs it contains.

Complex carbs are called complex because the body genuinely takes longer to break them down. This means that there will be a constant fuel source in your body, and you will experience a consistent stream of energy as you go about your day. You will have better energy levels, feel full for a more extended period of time, and have a longer chance to use the energy you put into your body.

Now, let's talk about what contains complex carbs.

The first thing is anything labeled "whole grain." When you buy bread, noodles, rice, and anything that happens to be a carb and bread-based product, look for that whole grain label. Often, this means that a simple substitution might be needed, but it will do the trick! This includes cereal too. Some cereals are based on simple carbs (which we will talk about in a minute), whereas some are based on complex carbs. Whole grain will be your key to discovering which is which!

Next is any sort of legume. These are a great source of protein as well as energy. Legumes are commonly known as beans. Now, certain beans aren't necessarily legumes. They are simple carbs that won't provide the same benefits. The bean types you can benefit from are listed below:

- Black beans

- Lima beans

- Soybeans

- Cranberry beans

- Pinto beans

- Lentils

- Red kidney beans

- Fava beans

- Garbanzo

- Yellow and green split peas

- Black-eyed peas

- Great northern beans

- Cannellini beans

- Mung beans

- Adzuki beans

There are plenty to choose from, as you can see. Many grocery stores will sell mixed beans by the bag.

Yet another excellent example of complex carbs is fruit. Fruit is a fantastic energy source, and as an added bonus, it's sweet, so you can easily convince your kiddo to have some.

Finally, starchy vegetables are complex carbohydrates, and your kiddo will probably enjoy these too. Starchy vegetables are usually root vegetables, and they include regular and sweet potatoes, beets, turnips, corn, carrots, and squash.

Lean Meats and Protein

Protein is essential to the body. From a young age, doctors stress the importance of protein in a child's diet. I've heard the phrase "you need to eat your protein to grow big and strong" multiple times, and it's true! Protein is actually essential for muscle growth. It also helps with the regeneration and building of cells within the body. Have you ever heard that your body cells are completely regenerated every seven years, and you are an entirely new person? Science has yet to back up this theory, but many acknowledge that this may be true, given that this process does occur (we just don't know at what rate). Finally, protein aids in enzyme and healthy bacteria production in the body. In short, it runs several essential functions that we need in order for our bodies to work correctly.

Lean proteins are generally better for you. At the same time, non-lean proteins (which tend to have more fat) are not harmful to you in small quantities. However, when they are consumed regularly over long periods, they can cause some issues, such as heart attacks, heart disease, strokes, high blood pressure, and diabetes. The proteins to keep limited include red meats such as beef, pork, lamb, and to a lesser extent, eggs.

Now, lean proteins include white meats such as chicken, turkey, and other bird-based meats, and it also includes fish and shellfish of all kinds. Tofu is a good source of lean protein, and so are legumes. Low-fat dairy like 2% milk, low-fat yogurts, cottage cheese, etc., and nuts are also on this list.

These foods will help your child's body keep up with their activity.

Fats (Well, Healthy Fats)

Much like our carbs, there are two types of fats you should keep your eye on. One is Saturated fat, and the other is unsaturated fat. Saturated fat is the bad one. Due to a series of processing that removes a lot of vitamins and minerals, it essentially adds weight to the poor person who is trying to enjoy their meal.

Baked and fried foods contain saturated fat, and processed meats contain saturated fat. Whole fat dairy (whole milk, whole yogurt, etc.) and solid cooking oils (packaged oils) contain this fat.

Now for the fun list! Unsaturated fat looks quite different, and it hasn't been over-processed, so it still has the essential things that children need. Fat helps the body break down the vitamins from food and supplements and puts them where it needs to go. The vitamins it concentrates on include vitamin A, vitamin D, vitamin E, and vitamin K.

Omega-3s are the fats to be on the lookout for. Due to their high demand, any foods that have been enriched with this fat are going to advertise it.

One common food that contains omega-3 includes fatty fish, and this is typically tuna and salmon. Another example is tree nuts (almonds, walnuts, hazelnuts, etc.). Avocados have been recently discovered to contain a good balance of fat, and you can find them anywhere. Finally, there are seeds, and Chia seeds, flax seeds, and pumpkin seeds are great examples that can help add healthy fats to your child's diet.

Vitamins and Minerals

While essential to every child's growth, children with ADHD further benefit from the regular inclusion of vitamins in their diet.

A very recent study shows that vitamins (referred to as micronutrients) stand a chance of improving symptoms of inattentive ADHD. This includes benefits for combined-type, and it can also help those with the hyperactive-impulsive type.

Along with this, there is something to keep an eye out for. Children with ADHD seem to run into trouble meeting their needs for iron and zinc levels.

The best protection against this is first to make sure your kiddo is taking their vitamins each day, and second, ensure that the vitamins they are taking include these things. Some other vitamins and minerals to be on the lookout for include vitamin B6, vitamin D, calcium, and magnesium. Along with making sure that they are taking their vitamins, you can double-check that they eat several different foods over the course of the day. Many vitamins naturally occur in food, so variety can increase your chances of getting it into your diet. Some foods to focus on have been on our lists above, including fruit, vegetables, whole grains, low-fat dairy, seeds and nuts, and fish.

Your kiddo, overall, should have a well-balanced diet. Doing so may not cure ADHD, but it can seriously help mitigate the symptoms.

Our bodies can only function at the rate they are fueled. This tends to hold true, no matter what age a person might be. When we add conditions like ADHD into the mix, the body might be trying to work overtime to make those brain connections. Not only will these foods help keep your child going, but a general regimen of eating right improves overall brain function and helps create more brain connections. At the very least, it will make things easier for your child.

With that being said, some foods will make ADHD symptoms worse (either slightly or by a lot). Next, we will discuss what those foods are and why they do what they do.

Foods That Your Child Should Avoid

Now we will cover things that are either bad for the developing body or seem to have an effect on ADHD symptoms. You don't necessarily have to cut these foods out of your diet, but it is highly recommended to limit them as much as possible.

Artificial Coloring

I'll admit, I was a bit surprised by this one. Artificial dyes and food colorings are very popular in America, arguably more so than in other countries. Accentuated color seems appealing until you realize that it's either heavily regulated or banned in many regions. This is because they don't really add to food and do a bit of unnecessary harm to the individual who consumes them.

These dyes are created by chemicals and can trigger hyperactivity and other ADHD symptoms.

Most candies (excluding some chocolates) are made with artificial dyes. But a wide range of other foods is too. Chips, dips and spreads, juices, bottled tea, and sometimes even items like bread or fries can contain dyes.

Do be on the lookout. Most ingredient lists won't say "artificial coloring" on the label, especially with the recent discoveries of how harmful these dyes are. Instead, they might say things like RED 40, YELLOW 6 (a popular one that is banned in Norway and Austria), BLUE 10, etc. Lookup any specific colors you see, as some are more harmful than others. Some might do relatively minor damage to you, while others are bad enough to be banned in some countries.

Your child does not have to forgo these dyes entirely. If it's a lovely weekend summer day and everyone's getting some fruit punch at the park, that's one thing. However, if it's right before a school day, that is another story.

Refined Sugars and Simple Carbohydrates

I have grouped refined sugar and simple carbs together because there is a lot of overlap in the food that contains them.

Again, refined sugar is very heavily processed, and it can do a lot of damage if consumed continuously over time.

Both refined sugar and simple carbohydrates have a lot of the same effects that red meat does, including leading to heart disease and attacks, strokes, type 2 diabetes, high blood pressure, and more. The difference, though, is that red meat still has protein benefits. Refined sugars and simple carbs do not, and these are processed so that everything beneficial about them is stripped away, except for the components that contain energy.

In refined sugars, these sugars and energies are running rampant through your child's system, making them hyper and giving them that sugar high.

The same is accurate for simple carbs, and it doesn't have the slow release that complex carbs do. It gives you energy and does it fast, but it takes it away as soon as your body has digested it. To make matters worse, when your body digests it quickly, any energy not used is stored as fat.

Refined sugars are often found in typical unhealthy foods like candies, snacks and chips, and bakery items.

You can find simple carbs in flour (white flour), white bread, white rice, regular noodles, as well as many other things out there. Whole wheat items are the ones that haven't been stripped and processed, which is why these are great labels to look for.

Again, these don't necessarily have to be cut out of a diet altogether, but it is best to limit them.

Caffeine

Caffeine can be especially hard if you have a teen on your hands.

ADHD is naturally something that messes with energy levels, meaning that they can sometimes be very high. Combining the two may get you a rocket ball of energy.

Another thing not to mess with is mixing caffeine with medication (at least without talking to a doctor). Many medications prescribed for ADHD are stimulants, and caffeine is also a stimulant. Combining the two can create quite a hyperactive person. It can also be dangerous, and it may cause severe anxiety and induce an anxiety or panic attack. Caffeine is also known to have adverse effects on the body when you drink a lot of it, and it can commonly affect the heart and your nervous system. Finally, it can cause a loss of appetite and insomnia (which is also a risk with medication).

Caffeine is harmless to the average person if they are not drinking a crazy amount. But in someone with ADHD, especially if they are taking medication, it can cause the body to go haywire.

Caffeine is not just in coffee either, and you can also find it in teas, sodas, some juices, and even things like chocolate.

Sample Diet and Best Tips

There are, of course, some tips that should be shared that can help you manage food intake and ADHD to lead to better symptoms. I want to share these with you, and I want to share a diet plan that is generally already catered to many of these tips.

Be On the Lookout For Sensitivities and Allergies

Children with ADHD seem more prone to having food sensitivities and allergies. Severe allergies are easy to spot and should be avoided at all costs, but some allergy symptoms are mild. Hives, if they are underclothes, are one example. Other things to watch for would be your child complaining about their mouth hurting or feeling numb, and this is a sign that they might be developing an allergy.

In a comparative example, a friend noticed this happen with cinnamon one year. She largely ignored when her mouth would go numb until she experienced an anaphylactic shock. It is scary to think about, but this can happen.

There are foods that cause sensitivities as well. If your child complains about an itchy mouth or an upset stomach, that is a sign of sensitivity. Your child's body may also reject the food through vomiting or diarrhea. Keep track of what foods cause this and see if you find a pattern. Given that it's more common in children with ADHD, it's something to be cautious about!

Balance and Routine

A healthy routine and balance have proven to be effective in helping those who have ADHD.

Having three balanced meals in a row, with a snack or two spaced in between, has proven effective in all age groups and with typical and atypical children.

Try to include at least two to three foods from the list above at each meal. Add fruit and whole grains at breakfast. Add protein and vegetables to their lunch, and the list goes on.

Another popular tip is to have a schedule for eating that your kiddo can stick to. It will help your kiddo out with the expectations, and routine always tends to help manage ADHD. Finally, skipping meals is not a good idea for children with ADHD. Children with ADHD tend to be very active, so skipping meals might lead to low blood sugar. If your child has easy access to snacks, it might be tempting to overcompensate their loss by snacking on junk food, which will likely lead to a very hyper child.

Have Things Prepared In Advance

We talked about meal prepping a little at the beginning of the chapter, and I will stress again that it can be helpful to maintain healthy eating. Another thing that can help you is preparing some healthy snacks and having them in easy grab reach. These can include fruits like apples, grapes, oranges, or strawberries, including vegetables like carrots, tomatoes, celery, or broccoli. Nuts are another excellent option, and having some whole wheat bread with a nut spread (peanut butter, almond butter, or hazelnut spread) is a great idea too. If your child is craving something sweeter or richer, these spreads can help with that too!

Children with ADHD tend to be constant balls of energy! Having things ready from the go is a little step to help you keep up!

Eliminate Slowly

We have talked about many different foods that might contribute to worsening ADHD symptoms. It may be tempting to remove all of these from your kiddo's diet immediately and get them started on healthier options. Here's the thing, though: your kiddo is used to these foods, and so is their body. Making such a sudden switch is likely to send them into a rage and send their body into a shock before it balances itself out again.

Try eliminating things one by one. Either make a plan or if your kiddo is old enough to understand the nuances of eating right, sit down and talk with them. Let them know why you think this will be a great idea. Let them know that you think this will be good for their ADHD and list all the benefits. Eliminate one food a week, and if your kiddo is old enough, let them make the schedule to give them an aspect of control.

Restriction

The restriction is for those kiddos who may have a lot of allergies or you suspect that other foods are affecting their ADHD.

I will add here that it is possible that certain foods that don't affect ADHD expression in other children do affect it in your children. This isn't highly researched, but each body is different, so this is an excellent way to test your theory if you suspect something.

With this idea, you cut their diet down to very basic foods. These are going to be hypoallergenic foods that won't cause any sort of thing in the body.

Stay with this for a few weeks (a month at most), and then start reintroducing some foods. Only introduce about one to two at a time so that if the body or brain experiences a decrease in function or there is an adverse reaction, you know the cause. Several diet guidelines out there can guide you on the minimum amount of foods needed to ensure that your child is satisfied both in terms of hunger and nutrition needs.

It is worth noting that this plan is best for older kids. For young children who don't quite understand everything about allergies and food sensitivities, this diet means potentially getting rid of foods they love, which is a great way to induce a meltdown.

Older children can keep track of what's going on in their bodies. Have them keep a log and track any changes (even embarrassing ones) that happen in their body so that you both can get an idea of what might be causing problems.

The only warning I can give for this tip is that it's going to be a process, and it should only be undertaken if you have concerns about how food might be affecting your child. If you have these concerns, this is a great way to put them to the test and find out what is going on!

Diet Idea: Mediterranean Eating Pattern

The Mediterranean diet is one that is always on the popular diet list, but it's never near the top. That's because it's not created by someone who intends to make money from it and, therefore, has little marketing power. That being said, it has proven beneficial to those who follow it.

The Mediterranean diet is based on the culture and food choices of those around the Mediterranean Sea. These cover people in regions of Spain, Greece, Italy, and Portugal.

Because of the sea, their primary source of food is fish and small game, and their land is rich enough not to need processing to increase the quantity of food they grow.

This diet includes every food I have listed above and appropriate limits for the food that can hurt those with ADHD. If you are looking for a guideline of how often your child should be consuming certain foods, the food pyramids built off this diet can help!

It was insane for me to learn how much food and a person's diet choices can affect the brain, and it was even crazier to understand that some foods actually could harm my kiddo.

Luckily, with the correct information, you can balance things out. With everything in effect to help manage ADHD, it can grow into something beautiful. You do not always need to feel like you are fighting ADHD, which we will discuss next.

Chapter Seven
ADHD Is a Superpower

Why is having ADHD viewed as such a horrible diagnosis? It seems that there are many people out there who see such a thing as something that talks about the very character of a young child. It is such a powerful label, yet it doesn't do much to describe your child at all. People with ADHD are brilliant. They are a powerhouse and a force to be reckoned with. Some of the greatest minds are thought to have had ADHD.

Today our world is designed and structured around the ability to sit still and work for long periods. Typical individuals shouldn't even be doing that, and frankly, the ADHD brain isn't designed for that, and it's designed for activity, action, and creativity.

There are several benefits to having ADHD. Many people with the diagnosis have said that they don't mind having it, and there are several famous names out there that have come out and said that they have ADHD.

In this chapter, I want to take some time to talk about the benefits of ADHD. They aren't talked about enough, and opening this discussion can help many people out there see how ADHD can lead to huge benefits.

Finally, I want to give you some examples of individuals we've all heard of who have ADHD. As your child grows, they might struggle. They might listen to negative messages telling them they aren't good enough or won't be successful. Let's see some real people that prove this wrong. I can help restore some faith.

Benefits

Hyperfocus

Have you ever seen someone with ADHD enter hyperfocus mode? Because it is incredible!

Hyperfocus is an incredible state where everything else in the world fades into the background. It is just you and the thing you are working on. The end result is work that is not only complete but of high quality. Hyper-focusing can help some people with ADHD get away with procrastination while they are in school. But once they leave the education institution and are doing something they love, they have a real chance to do something unique with their hyper-focusing skills.

Engaging hyperfocus involves key elements. A looming deadline can absolutely engage hyperfocus, but how close to the deadline depends on how interesting the task is. Speaking of which, another thing that can engage hyperfocus is an exciting task. For some out there, it does not matter how big or complicated the task is; if they are interested, then the job will get done in just a moment.

Hyperfocus cannot be engaged on demand, although it would be cool if it could be. That being said, many professionals out there have a few strategies that help them lock it in. These strategies are specific to how their brains work and help them get things done! Can you think of any strategy that might have worked for your kiddo in the past?

Resilience

Think about this. Your child is facing many problems each day as a result of having ADHD. In order to move past these obstacles, children have to engage in problem-solving techniques and ideas, which naturally lead to better problem-solving skills down the line.

This is also true for building resilience. Children with ADHD do not have an easy world to face, but they do it every day. Even teachers in public schools note that children who have ADHD tend to be more resilient than others.

Such resiliency and problem-solving skills can take them so far in life. Many jobs look for these skills. Owning your own business or being an inventor requires such prowess.

I am not here to glamourize the process of getting them, but at the finish line, there are many amazing things to be said about these skills.

Creative and Outside-the-Box Thinking

Here is another area where ADHD kids excel. You've probably seen this yourself with your little one.

Children with ADHD tend to be more creative. This does show up in art forms, but it is also present in their ways of thinking about the world.

Creativity is a beautiful trait to have. It brings so much more to the world, and it allows your child a chance to build things and give something to the world while having something to share with others.

The same is very true for those who wish to think outside of the box. The world has too many people who can't do so. So many people look to outside-the-box thinkers to solve problems.

Again, both creativity and problem-solving go a long way in terms of being an adult and making money for yourself. Imagine what they can do later if your kiddo can develop these skills.

Conversationalist

Here is my next question for you! Have you ever had a conversation with an adult with ADHD? You probably have, but how in-depth did it go?

People with ADHD, especially adults with ADHD, know how to have a great conversation. This doesn't just mean that they can talk. They know how to make a conversation interesting, they know how to make it cover every topic under the sun, and they know how to keep you entertained and engaged.

Furthermore, people with ADHD have shown in studies to be able to pick up on the moods of others at an easier rate than those without. This means that they can read the room first, and going into a sudden situation is something they can pick up on. They may also be able to sit with someone looking to buy something from them and be able to read the person pretty well.

Again, when it comes to the adult world, the possibilities with these skills are endless.

Spontaneous Ideas

In childhood, it is called impulsivity. It's sadly fair to do this, as young children don't quite know that they are vulnerable to injury, and they tend to do things that might get them injured.

As an adult, though, we tend to have a grasp on the fact that jumping off a building to fly is a bad idea.

For typical adults, this perception gets even more narrow. That means that we might be less likely to diverge off the path or try new things. That's not always true for someone with ADHD. They are likely to try new things. This might mean they try sushi, skydiving, or meeting with a new client, and when they realize their current strategy isn't working, they change it up.

These aren't just great for one's career, but spontaneous ideas also bring about a great deal of life satisfaction.

Consistent Energy

People with ADHD can keep up with the busy world! Whereas a typical individual might struggle, someone with ADHD can be energized at most moments.

Again, this isn't just great for the working world, but imagine doing your job all day and still coming home giddy with energy to do something that you are excited about. It's exhilarating to think about, isn't it?

ADHD will sometimes look like struggling in this crazy world where so many crazy things are happening at once that you don't know what to do. It might sometimes look like getting overwhelmed and burnt out. It sometimes feels like there is so much going on in your head at once, and you don't know how to stop it, yet if it doesn't stop soon, you are going to scream.

It can also look like someone who has suddenly hunkered down to produce fantastic work. It can look like someone who is creative and thinks outside the box. It's breaking down social walls and keeping everything together and entertained. ADHD is so many things wrapped into one package.

I understand that you and your kiddo are probably struggling a bit, and I offer this to show you that ADHD isn't the end. There are many great things about it, and next, we are going to talk about how to leverage these abilities.

How to Make the Most Out of This

Top Tips

Many of the skills mentioned will serve them well in adulthood, so long as they know how to use them! Here are some ways to practice early!

Hyperfocus can become an early practice. Help your child find some of their big interests. Foster them and give them time and space to work on these interests. The results of this might surprise you!

Resilience will foster itself naturally, but having low self-esteem can hinder this. If you start to notice that your child's self-esteem is dropping, try doing some self-esteem work to bring it back up. When they face challenging situations and cope well, it can build resilience. If they do not manage well, or something in their coping strategy fails, it can lead to low self-esteem. Should their coping strategy fail, a great way to build resilience and prevent a self-esteem plummet is to sit down with them and make a plan for next time. Think about what can be done differently. Is there a new strategy to try? This preparation has them ready for next time rather than thinking they cannot handle something.

Creativity can be fostered in much the same way that hyperfocus can. Give them space, materials, and time, and let them explore their interests. The more opportunity we have to use our brains for creativity, the more it will foster and develop.

Look into opportunities your child can jump into for those conversational skills. As children enter high school, there will be opportunities like student government, debate, the newspaper, and more! These are great places for those conversational skills to be put to the test. With supervision, you also might let your child give social media a try if they are interested.

As children share their spontaneous ideas with you, consider them. Try not to say no too quickly when your kiddo shares a vision. Let them entertain their new ideas.

People with ADHD can grow up to be unique and talented human beings. It's going to be interesting to see what they might do next!

Management Ideas

How do you keep ADHD in check with the aforementioned abilities? How do you let them flourish but still restrain yourself enough so that you don't blow people away?

First things first! Have a to-do list, a planner, or something that will help them keep track. I know I've mentioned it before, and it's such a common tip, but trust me, it really helps! It gives them a visual reminder and helps them know what to do next and plan out their day.

The next suggestion is to time tasks. If you have ten things to get done today, you don't have time to hyperfocus on one of them and do it perfectly. That's where time limits come in. Setting a timer on your phone can help you know that it's time to switch to another task.

ADHD superpowers enable great success when kiddos know how to leverage them properly!

Celebrities

Children always need positive role models in their lives. This is something that a child can look up to. A role model is someone that they want to be like. Many celebrities and professionals have talked about having ADHD. Here are a few you should let your kiddo know about. Give your kid a chance to find someone whom they might see as like them that they can admire.

Simone Biles

Simone Biles has been a household name for quite some time for all of the little gymnasts out there. Her medical history was leaked, including the medications she took. She responded honestly and with no shame that her medications were there to treat her for ADHD.

The American gymnastic champion has won nearly 20 gold medals. This is someone that your child can look up to, not only for strength but as a great example of when it's time to pull back. Biles received mixed reactions about withdrawing from part of the Olympics in 2021, but she has stood by her decision as it was, in fact, for her health.

Justin Timberlake

Justin Timberlake has done a lot in the music world. Of course, some hits that come to mind are "Sexyback" and "Can't stop the feeling" from Trolls. Given his wide range, he is a great role model to kids of all ages with ADHD, which he mentioned having in one of his interviews.

Adam Levine

Adam Levine has been vocal about his struggles with ADHD for a long time. He has made it a point, to be honest when talking about ADHD in many interviews and sharing his story, including the highs and lows of having it.

Today, Levine works as one of the coaches on The Voice and is the lead singer of Maroon 5.

Channing Tatum

Here is another individual who hasn't let anything stop him. Channing Tatum's acting credit list is probably as long as a CVS receipt, something he accomplished with ADHD. He has talked about what it's like to have ADHD as a child, and it is something your child might find very relatable!

Emma Watson

What hasn't Emma Watson done with her life? Many young girls idolize young Hermione and her love of books and learning (Seriously, why wasn't she in Ravenclaw again?). The real-life Emma Watson has added a lot more acting credits to her name, including a very notable role as Belle in Beauty and the Beast. And to top it off, she's gotten a degree at Brown University (one of the hardest schools to get into in America) and serves as a United Nations ambassador. Watson still has a lot of life ahead of her, so for those who see her as a role model, it will be interesting to see what she does next!

Micheal Phelps

Micheal Phelps and Biles have a very similar story. Like Biles, Phelps has dedicated his career to being an American olympian athlete. In total, he has won about 23 gold medals, all thanks to his swimming skills. Both he and his mother have talked about his ADHD, saying that swimming has been something in his life that brought him to focus and control. If you have a kiddo struggling right now who is into sports, you never know. At the very least, this could be a model of inspiration for them.

Lisa Ling

There are many reasons that both you and your child could relate to Lisa Ling. Ling is a journalist and often tackles big projects. Her latest was "Our America with Lisa Ling." In it, Ling covered some ADHD topics. Now, if you have ever had a "wait a minute" moment in your life, you might relate to Ling. In doing this project, she noticed several parallels. She got her ADHD diagnosis shortly afterward. Ling is a fantastic example to your kiddo as someone who goes for what she wants and doesn't let the world stop her. Her recent discovery of ADHD and having to deal with this new information suddenly might seem like a familiar story to you.

Will.i.am

Music is a popular path for many with ADHD, and Will.i.am has taken the time to highlight that. He has stated in several interviews that music has helped him cope with ADHD symptoms, among other things, and that when he's in the zone, it clicks. Does your kiddo relate?

Scott Kelly

Many of our examples cover people you might see on a TV screen. Scott Kelly might have been on TV at multiple points in his life, but not the same way the others have.

Growing up, Scott Kelly mentions that his school experience was a mirror image of what someone with ADHD would go through, but they didn't have the diagnosis, so he went undiagnosed. What made him finally get on track was his love for all things space-based. Kelly was able to motivate himself to hyperfocus on school enough to go on and become an astronaut. Today, he is working on getting humans to Mars.

Science is a beautiful yet complicated field. If your little one seems to have a pension for it, this is a great person to point to. Everyone is capable of great things, after all.

Ty Pennington

Some kids rearrange their room 17 times in one year to find the best functionality. If this is your kiddo, they might relate to Ty Pennington.

Pennington is an interior decorator on the show Extreme Makeover: Home Edition. His ADHD is expressed a lot in his job, and he, his mother, his coworkers, and his customers all attest that it is making him very successful.

Karina Smirnoff

Dancing is a popular sport with people everywhere, and many young children enjoy themselves in their dance classes.

If your little one is a dancer, and they get the opportunity to watch Dancing With the Stars, point out Karina Smirnoff. Like many girls with ADHD, this star was diagnosed as an adult. In an interview, she said that her ADHD gives her a lot of energy, and it all goes to her amazing dancing.

Johnny Depp

Depp is an actor who has worn many hats. Literally. Nearly every eccentric children's movie features Johnny Depp, and Depp is Willy Wonka, the Mad Hatter, Captain Jack Sparrow, and more. Not only is it amazing that he has done so much with his life, but he is always on a child's screen.

Richard Branson

Moving away from the stage, it's important to talk about how well people with ADHD can do in the business world. Our first shining example is Sir Richard Branson. His business, Virgin Brand, is everywhere, and it is involved in the health sector, travel sector, banking, space, cell phones, music, etc. Branson has been very public about ADHD, yet he is worth billions today.

Jamie Oliver

Does the name Jamie Oliver sound familiar? If you are anywhere near the UK food scene, it probably will. Oliver is one of the most decorated chefs in the UK, winning awards for his accomplishments. He has been honest about having ADHD, and it doesn't seem to slow him down!

Bill Gates

I absolutely had to throw this name in here. Bill Gates invented Microsoft. That sentence alone speaks for itself. However, his journey wasn't an easy one and included dropping out of Harvard. Sometimes unique ideas can be constrained in school, making it hard to know what you might be capable of. If your kiddo is struggling, as many do, let them know that they don't have to be exceptional in a classroom to succeed in life. Many people don't do it that way.

Role models are always crucial to younger kids. They can give them a chance to have something to look up to, an example to follow, or even just a way to know that it's going to be okay on bad days.

ADHD isn't a negative thing. There are negative symptoms, but the rewired brain is full of potential. These are some people who were able to lock on it, and your kiddo might be able to do this as well!

Chapter Eight

Teaching Your Child Life Skills

At the end of the day, the goal of raising children is to turn them into happy and successful adults. That sounds great. Right?

ADHD can feel like it puts a bit of a dampener on that, understandably. Hopefully, the last chapter illustrates that might not be the case. Still, there is likely a way to go, and having superpowers with their ADHD doesn't mean they can skip out on basic life skills. So, what does that look like when your kiddo has ADHD?

Activities and Strategies That Can Help

A list for you!

Lists don't just help those who suffer from ADHD! Trying to organize all of the skills someone needs to learn throughout their childhood can feel like a monumental task. If you feel overwhelmed about it, that's understandable. Creating lists can help you get this in front of you in order to develop a plan of what you want to work on.

If you're struggling to find some examples of practical tasks for your kiddo, many online resources outline the age-appropriateness of specific duties.

Once you have a list, give your kiddo an opportunity to choose ones they want to work on first, as it might help with motivation!

Create Activities Out of It

There are many adulting skills that can be fun to learn. One example is cooking, and another is gardening, painting, and decorating are even better examples. All of these can be made into a game or at least made fun.

Let your child cook a dish as long as they are old enough. But, do not stop there. Let them choose the ingredients and pick out the groceries. By following the process, they have more control, and they learn a couple of skills along the way.

Let your child attend to a small garden. Box gardens are a great start. Finally, when it is needed, let them help redecorate their room.

Pay More Attention To What's Working

This one is hard. We want children to know how to do something perfectly. However, if we are too critical from the get-go, they may stop trying altogether. As they start the new task, focus on the things they are doing correctly. Complement those things and leave the issues at the moment. If, after a few months, there isn't much improvement, try moving to a certain phrasing in constructive criticism. As silly as it might sound, avoid using "but." For example, try not to say, "you did really well at this, but...". Instead, try "wow, we're doing really well with this. Parts' A,' and 'B' looks amazing, and we're just missing a tiny part on task 'C.'". This phrasing uses 'and' instead of 'but,' and it points out the issue without being too critical. For children who are struggling with a task, this can help them know what to improve on without being a hit to their motivation.

Achievement Chart

Are you working on a new task right now? Another way to help your child grow in skills without criticism is to have a chart where they move up as their performance improves. This also can help them understand what they still need to work on. Perhaps there is a small prize or the opportunity to do something fun at the end of the day. Charts are also visual, meaning that kiddos with ADHD will have a better time remembering each time they do the task rather than trying to remember your feedback from last time.

Start With Organization Skills ASAP

Generally, the ADHD brain is not the most organized. Now, that's fine, but what sits in our brain may spill into our physical world. Luckily, organization skills can be taught very early and are likely to stick if you do so. When you teach your kiddo about organization skills, let them know that it doesn't have to be perfect, and it just has to make sense to them.

If you are trying to implement this now, start by getting them excited. You can find some great organization pieces at local craft stores, Walmart, Target, a dollar store, and more! Let them pick some items out that they can make use of! Once that's done, help them create a system. Using labels can help it be more visually apparent as well! As they adjust to having an organizational system, try to check in with them about it. See how it's working, how well they are sticking to it, and if there is anything that can be done to improve the system.

Timers

Distractions tend to be around every corner when you have ADHD. You might have given your child the task of sweeping the kitchen and what you've found is that your kiddo made one or two strokes with the broom and is now watching a hummingbird outside (hey, hummingbirds are cool, but we need to stay on task). One thing that can help is a visual timer. Knowing that chores have to be done at a specific time can help prevent distractions, and on really good days, it can potentially engage hyperfocus.

Be Hands-On

The final thing for this section is to be as hands-on as possible. Children with ADHD generally don't do well when they are just told something, and they need further instruction in the form of visual cues and potentially even the chance to do it with you if that is possible.

Our next set of strategies is for those with older kids!

Teenage Based Strategies

The teenage years can be a scary time, especially if your teen has ADHD. Along with going through this development time, you have to think about another frightening thing. Becoming an adult is right around the corner, and as you look at your 13-year-old or even your 16-year-old, it can be hard to imagine. If that thought makes you panic, do not fret. A lot will happen in these next couple of years, and we are going to be here with some tips to help you get through it!

Organization

With teens, organization isn't just about space anymore. Not only do they need to know about organizing their rooms and personal belongings, but knowing how to organize a schedule is going to become a big deal as well! A lot of the same steps will translate. Make it fun. Get a physical planner, or download an online app that can help them! To make it something they can follow visually, use color filters online, or get some colorful pens and highlighters!

Independence

There is going to be a love-hate relationship on all sides when it comes to independence. Some simple forms of cutting off dependence will be things like not being the one to wake them up for school or remind them to do their homework or tell them to do their chores. You might move them over to preparing their own lunch and possibly another meal during the week, and it may be doing their own laundry. Little things like this, where you typically handle the work, will now be up to them. It's a good idea to get the skill in while you are still close by to answer questions.

I know that it is going to be hard to let them do these things, especially when they forget, but these are the things that will help them in life. And when they forget or fail to do something, right now, they are under your roof so that you can help them, and the consequences are minimal.

The Financial Deal

One trait of ADHD is impulsivity, and let's be honest, that can be really bad for a person's budget. Financial intelligence is something they are better to learn under your roof rather than in the world. First of all, if your teen is able to secure a part-time job, particularly one that is active, it can give them a chance to experience structure. If your teen gets to this point, get a hold of some things that will require them to keep a monthly budget. Some basics are car insurance, gas, and a phone bill. Now, you might want to add on a fun thing or two; it could be a streaming service, for example. One great idea that might cater to your child's interests is subscription boxes. These can be whatever you want (books, art supplies, tea, or even things like snacks from across the world). These things give your kiddo something to look forward to while, at the same time, helping them balance a budget. In order to keep the fun stuff, they will need to be financially responsible.

Encourage Various Relationships

Your child should know what a healthy dating relationship is like, and if they naturally start dating someone while still living with you, here is an excellent opportunity to teach them. This also holds true for friendships, family relationships, if there are any diverse examples, and working relationships if they happen to hold a part-time job.

Getting an idea of what relationships should look like now is going to be an excellent idea for any teen, but especially one with any kind of disability. Unfortunately, people with disabilities are more likely to be taken advantage of by other people, so it's great for them to know what a healthy relationship and health boundaries look like.

A Natural Course Of Action

I remember when I woke up late for school, I rushed around to get everything ready and begged my mom to drive me. She did while letting me know that she was disappointed in me and that I was in trouble for sleeping in.

First of all, we all make human mistakes. My mom didn't have to tell me she was disappointed in me. I was already disappointed in myself, and I had let the mistake happen. Thanks to her, I was on time at least.

For a child with ADHD (or any child), this doesn't help much. When things like this happen, there isn't a need to get mad. They likely already know that something is wrong, and in cases like sleeping in, many people silently go through it in their head about what they should do next time to avoid this.

Now, without saying anything, what is going to help the lesson sink in? Letting the natural course of events take place will. If your child is late walking out the door, they are late to school. As harsh as it sounds, wish them luck and send them on their way. Knowing the direct result of the actions will help them avoid the mistake next time. You don't have to be into math to see it.

The Skills

All of the little tips and tricks we have discussed above (for children young and old) will become very important right here!

Increasing Independence

In teens, we mentioned that there are certain things that they might want to take charge of, but what does this look like for young children? There is a certain level of recommended independence and autonomy at each age that a little one has. Following guidance on this can help ensure that your child is ready to enter the real world.

Time

Again, we talked about this with teens, but it applies to kiddos as well, and I want to address that here. Young children will not always understand what time is and how long certain things might take. For example, if they have a homework assignment that they need to do before an extracurricular activity, they might put it off until the last second. Things like this are when tools like timers and natural consequences come into play so that it helps your child understand what time looks like and how much of it they have.

Saving

Financial building blocks are also best taught in stages. Your teen may be paying for a subscription, but your child may know of a toy they want. Children can learn the power of saving starting at a very young age. If there is something that they want, saving up their allowance is a great way to get it and learn while they are at it!

Taking Charge of Their Meds

We haven't talked much about medication purely because that's a conversation that doctors like to have. If your child does take medication, one day, they are going to have to take it on their own. As they get older, try to slowly guide them to where they are in charge of making sure that they take their medications.

Decision-Making Power

Being impulsive is great for a sudden road trip, trying a new restaurant, or a crazy activity like skydiving. It's not okay for ditching class, speeding, or getting in trouble for drinking at a young age.

This area needs additional focus for the lives of those with ADHD. Making decisions is something they are going to do all of their lives, and having a process together to make good ones is going to help!

There are so many skills out there for adulthood, and it's our job to prepare our kids, no matter what. ADHD might mean that you require some new approaches, but you still got this!

Conclusion

I want to reiterate that I understand how this all feels, and I've been in many of the same positions that you are in right now. Thankfully, I found that a lot of these tips were able to work for my daughter and me.

To date, we are not sure what exactly causes ADHD, but we have a few ideas. It's believed to be located in the prefrontal cortex, where the function of many issues inhibited by ADHD tends to occur. Serotonin production seems to have a role in it as well. Serotonin acts as our motivation chemical, and having it not be adequately produced can create a lot of issues with getting tasks done in a timely manner, something that a lot of people with ADHD struggle with.

There are three identified types of ADHD. Inattentive ADHD has more to do with paying attention to the world around them and is more common in girls. Hyperactive-impulsive ADHD involves impulse control, trouble sitting, hyperactivity, and more. This one is more common in boys. Meanwhile, combined-type ADHD sort of meshes the two together, and it's slightly more common in boys than in girls.

There are some different conditions that relate to ADHD. These range from learning disabilities to emotional disorders. Chapter 2 goes into a lot of details about these. Knowing what signs to look for can help you and your kiddo catch and diagnose these early, which will help you to adjust to this new diagnosis and plan some strategies.

A common thing that many parents run into regarding the child and ADHD is severe emotional outbursts. When someone with a typical brain gets angry, their anger flares up, and they might have a tiny moment where they yell at someone, but then the anger signal will fade away. This isn't true for someone with ADHD. Chemicals create emotions in the brain, and sometimes, that anger signal doesn't fade. It just keeps going, flooding your child with too much n emotion that they don't quite know how to control. It is essential to recognize that this isn't your kiddo's fault when this happens. They really can't control these mechanisms in their brain. During the meltdown, it's often best to let them have their moment. Anything said during that point might not be remembered, or it might enrage them further. Trying to punish this behavior will not affect a child with ADHD. There are some other, different strategies that might make a difference, though.

Speaking of punishment and discipline, there are methods that are ideally suited for those who have ADHD, but there are many that are not. Punishment methods may make the problem worse in the long run, and discipline strategies will only work when the behavior is intentional, which a lot of the behaviors displayed in someone with ADHD aren't. There are ways to make sure they understand the message and help them move past incidents and outbursts in a positive and productive manner.

Diet and exercise are important to everyone, but they can have a unique effect on people with ADHD. Exercise can be especially helpful to someone who is hyperactive. Diet plays a significant role in their health, and having a good diet can manage some ADHD symptoms.

The final thing I want to stress in this book is that ADHD is not all bad. People with ADHD have a specific skill set that allows them to be very productive in this world. Not only that, but they seem to be fantastic at coming up with new things and ideas that bring them success. As they grow and develop, allowing them to take full advantage of the things that their ADHD can do for them can help them grow up to be unique and successful human beings.

Life Skills For Your ADHD Teen

Coping Skills and Life Lessons to Prepare Your Teen for The Emotional World Ahead

Kenneth Harvey

Introduction

I want you to imagine, for a moment, an average day in Jennifer's life. Jennifer is the mother of sixteen-year-old Trinity. In Jennifer's eyes, Trinity is perfect, and she is truly sweet and caring. She's managed to make money by making and selling jewelry and has an absolutely magnetic personality.

Trinity also has ADHD, and that has contributed to several issues that worry Jennifer. As she goes downstairs, she can't help but notice that Trinity is in the same clothes as yesterday and hasn't brushed her hair. Jennifer doesn't have to ask to know that she didn't take a shower or brush her teeth. Trinity is on her phone, waiting to flip a pancake. Jennifer jumps in to flip it after starting to smell it burn. Even though the pancake is black, Trinity rolls her eyes. She counters with a "mom, it's fine. I can cook for myself!"

After putting the issue to rest and enjoying breakfast, Trinity rushes around, grabbing homework, keys, and other things she knows she will need. Jennifer sighs and rubs her eyes, and this was something she was supposed to have done last night.

"Where's your lunch?" she has to ask. Trinity stops, shrugs and says she will pick something up to go from the nearest chain coffee shop. She shrugs off her mother's concerns about her having enough money for that.

Finally, they both head out the door. Jennifer notices that Trinity is entering the school into google maps before she takes off. While Jennifer knows that she will at least make it to school, she worries. Trinity has been going to the same school this whole time, and she's been driving for over a month. How does she not know the way?

During the day, Jennifer gets a notification that Trinity was late to her homeroom. The teacher took particular offense. After all, she was clearly late because she went to get coffee. She also got a text from her daughter, asking to grab a piece of homework that she'd forgotten.

Jennifer loved her daughter and knew that she'd make the world a better place, but she was really worried. Her daughter was sixteen, and there were still some critical life skills that she seemed to lack. How did she make sure that her daughter got those skills before she left? Trinity was already talking about college, so it was only a matter of time.

To Jennifer, it felt like there were so many things to go over in such a short amount of time, and she didn't know where to start. On the one hand, she knew that her daughter had the hardcore skills to make it in life. Her personality would take her far. She had passion, and heck, she even had her own little business together. But what about some of the softer things and the essential skills that one needs. Trinity can't afford to always grab something from the nearest coffee shop for a meal. She won't be there when the food is burning. She won't be there if Trinity needs someone to run her the homework. And that just touched on a couple of the issues she noticed today. What should she do?

The number of things we need to teach our little ones as they grow into adults can feel overwhelming. As we go through life, the world isn't going to care about whether you have attention-deficit/hyperactivity disorder (ADHD) or you don't. As cold as it is to say, it is the reality that we find ourselves in, and our kids will find themselves there too. It's our job as parents to worry about how they will do and teach them what they need to know.

In the future, our kids will know how to present themselves. They will learn how to keep themselves healthy. They will understand how to plan and manage things, and they will be able to remember everything as they walk out the door. The key is for us to give that guidance while they still live under our roof and not wait for the world to provide them with that guidance first.

There are many books out there that talk about how to give these skills to your teen. It talks about how to teach them to do things they will need to know, and it often outlines strategies you can use. The trouble with these books is that they are based on teens who don't have ADHD. Therefore, many of the teaching strategies may not work.

This book is designed to help with precisely that. I want to give you strategies that will work with your soon-to-be adult, and I also want to take the chance to highlight some unique adulting struggles that someone with ADHD might face. I know that it can feel frustrating when you have this monumental task ahead of you, and while some people have many resources to combat this problem, it seems you have relatively few.

I started this journey when there was even less information about ADHD than there is now. My daughter was diagnosed at a young age, and like you, I wanted to be there for her and support her. Most importantly, I didn't want her to leave my house without knowing how to be a functional adult with the ability to aim for her dreams.

With no resources readily available, I dove in deep. I did research, and I attended other classes. I got to know parents who also have children with ADHD and were also trying to raise children that could thrive in the world ahead of them. This has all amounted to over ten years of experience studying and learning from other parents, and I want to share my knowledge. I'm excited to pass on my knowledge in a way so that everyone can access it. Information about

ADHD and how to handle it while still raising successful human beings shouldn't be so hard to come by.

We're going to start this book with the basics. Self-care is vital but easy to neglect, especially when you have ADHD.

Chapter one
Self Care and Grooming

If your kiddo has ADHD, then this is probably a battle you've been at for a long time. Taking care of one's personal hygiene doesn't come naturally to many people and can be time-consuming and annoying. For someone with ADHD, it still takes long enough to do these tasks.

When you and your kiddo talk about personal hygiene, you've probably heard them mention that it just takes too much time and they'd rather be doing other things. You've also probably heard that no one is going to notice or really care, so why should they bother? This might be especially true if they plan to be home that day.

The other things you hear might relate to sensory issues or issues with cleanliness, which is common for someone with ADHD.

Jennifer knows that some of Trinity's complaints are that the toothpaste is too spicy, showers are too hot, and conversely, getting out of the water is too cold.

Finally, there is the tell-tale "I forgot," which may or may not be true.

Whatever the case, hygiene is important in making sure that they are presentable to the world, and more importantly, it keeps us from getting sick.

So, how do we make sure that our kids can really implement good hygiene practices before they leave the nest?

General Hygiene Tips and Tricks

Area 1: Brushing Your Teeth

Tip: Technology

It's the 21st century, so the fact that technology comes into play when we brush our teeth shouldn't be a surprise to me... but it is.

For parents with kids that really struggle, there are toothbrushes that connect to apps, which will help remind your teen that their teeth need to be brushed, time them and track how they are doing in getting every side brushed. This tech can absolutely help keep them on top of things!

It's also expensive! Some similar things you can do is have them make use of their phone to track how long they are brushing their teeth, and they can further divide the time if they aren't getting their sides evenly. Using a habit tracker can also encourage them to get their teeth brushed. There are simple ones and more complex ones that have you take care of something like a plant or penguin based on your completion of daily tasks.

Area 2: Caring For Your Body

Tip: Make it Visual

This works for just about anything. Having visual charts, rather than having something written out, can make a big difference in how things are processed. Simply put, you don't have to read a line of text to remember what's going on.

You can have a visual chart for showers, teeth brushing, face and hair care, and more. Furthermore, these schedules can be made by you and your teen, which can add to the willingness to follow if they are artistically inclined. You can also print out a simple one on Pinterest, or many sights make buyable versions. Whatever best helps you and your teen is your best bet!

Tip: Ask Them To Tell You What to Do... Backward

Have you ever had a tough test that you needed to memorize something for, so, in order to nail it, you memorize the process backward (fun fact: my teacher had us do this for the photosynthesis cycle)? You can do this with hygiene practices to help them remember. If they are struggling, go over the process with them a few times. Have them write it down in the correct order, then ask them to recite what they've just been taught backward. It's okay if it takes several tries, but typically, if you can do something backward, then it will work in the opposite direction too!

Tip: Repetition

One thing we will talk about a lot in this book is the process of natural consequences. Children with ADHD rarely learn the "why" of important behaviors when punishment is used. In fact, punishment may get you what has been termed as "instant obedience," but it will rarely get you what you really want, which is long-term learning. Punishment may even lead to an explosion later on, as children with ADHD don't have the best regulation abilities. This is something we want to avoid.

On the other hand, natural consequences illustrate a cause-and-effect relationship that the child can hold on to. In this case, the cause might be that they didn't properly shower or brush their teeth, and they need to be clean, so the effect is that they have to do it again.

If one of your teens' complaints is that it takes too long, then this lesson is going to stick fast.

Now, this might not work as well on older teens, and if it's still a struggle, it might be good to switch to a new tactic.

The effects of long-term lack of care are warned about in doctor and dentist offices, and the information is readily available online. Please share it with your teen, and let them know that there are reasons that personal care is essential and that, while it's annoying, it needs to be practiced.

Tip: Acknowledge Where the Difficulties Lay

No one likes being told that they aren't keeping up with their hygiene, especially when they are teenagers. It can result in some self-esteem issues, which is something that those with ADHD are more prone to. Remind them that, yes, it is just their ADHD getting in the way. It's okay for them to need more time to focus on it, and it's expected. There are still some things that they can do better than others because of their ADHD, and this might just be a struggling area.

Take Trinity, for example. She is, admittedly, one of the few students in her class that struggle with hygiene. But, every single one of her teachers has mentioned that she is animated. She's interesting to talk to and listen to, and she is one of the best presenters in her class. To top it all off, Trinity is building her own small business at age 18. How many teens do you know fit that?

Your teen might be annoyed that they have to pull away from something they were working on that they found really interesting. Acknowledge that as a valid feeling. It may not change the outcome of the situation, but it sucks!

Validate their issues with their senses. We may still have to shower, but maybe it really is too hot or too cold. If that's what they say, then try to work on strategies that help them reduce this issue.

In Trinity's case, she found the toothpaste her mom bought to be "too spicy." The minty flavor was too strong, and it hurt her mouth. Trinity's mom decided to switch brands for her, and she instantly noticed that the complaints all but stopped.

Finally, there's an important distinction to be made between actually being lazy or just having ADHD. When you have ADHD, you might not want to shower because of the reasons we just talked about, it could be because you are busy, or it could be something else entirely. It's rarely because a person is lazy. Making that distinction can be very preventative when it comes to fighting against low self-esteem.

What Problems Might Be Causing the Issue?

You will probably get an answer whenever you ask why they might not make hygiene practices a regular habit. The question is, is it the answer you need or the one they want you to hear?

There are many reasons why they might choose not to have a shower or brush their teeth. Let's take a look at some of the more common causes that we find when we dig deeper.

The Lack of Dopamine

The brain of someone with ADHD doesn't have as much dopamine as an average person. Dopamine is what is needed for the brain to function, and it's essentially the chemical that controls our motivation. When it comes to performing hygiene functions, dopamine will be pretty low. This alone is likely a huge part of your battle.

There are some ways you can replace that dopamine. Rewards are the most obvious way to do it. Creating a system where their efforts are rewarded can increase dopamine levels significantly. Rewards can be as simple as a piece of candy, a dollar, or a promise to play their favorite game. Each child will be different. See about sitting down and talking to yours about what might work for them.

Relating to dopamine deficiency is depression. Dopamine is also one of the chemicals responsible for happiness; a severe lack of it can lead to depression. When dealing with depression, not only is the brain struggling to create dopamine at a certain level, but it's also struggling to replenish it, and even risk-taking behaviors may not give a hit.

At this point, rewards might not help. Keep an eye out for depressive symptoms. When they last longer than two weeks and impact a person's daily functioning and overall quality of life, then they are said to have clinical depression.

In these cases, seeking help from a professional can make all of the difference! They can help you come up with strategies for routines and depression management. If needed, they can also recommend medication that can help!

Having a Set Schedule

Ask yourself, what does having a set schedule do for you?

For many of us, it creates balance. It helps us know what is going on next in our day, and it helps us make sure we get everything done.

Imagine, for a moment, not having any kind of schedule and finding sticking to them nearly impossible. This is often a huge struggle for those with ADHD. Their brain doesn't naturally stick to a schedule, making it very hard to stick with a plan in their day, and this includes making time for general hygiene practices.

When dealing with this, someone with ADHD isn't likely to make brushing their teeth or getting a shower their top priority.

When helping someone with ADHD create a schedule, it should first be in a place they check daily. A planner will work if they are likely to look at it. Other places include their bedroom wall, the fridge in the kitchen, or the lock screen of their phone, tablet, or computer. Making these schedules visual, instead of writing them out, will also make them easier to follow. The schedule should also include things they want to do to motivate them to stick to it. Finally, the schedules should be as simple as possible so that they are easy to read.

Lack Of Attention To the Clock

We might all have days when we don't pay attention to the clock and lose track of time. Someone with ADHD is much more prone to this than we might be. They may be in a phase of distraction, or they may be hyper-focused. Either way, it might be hours before they check the clock again.

In the case of your teen, they might get started on either their homework or another project. They get a good groove going, and all of a sudden, it's 10 p.m. They know they should shower and brush their teeth, but they are tired, so they go straight to bed.

It can be difficult to interrupt your child when they have a good flow going, especially when it's what they are supposed to do. That being said, it is important to ensure your child is doing regular hygiene practices to build a strong habit.

In this case, having timers set on their phone will make them look at the clock and remind them that it's time to step away from work and toward the shower.

If your teen has a tendency just to turn off the reminder and continue working, then you can set the timer on your phone or be mindful of the time and remind them about 15 minutes after the timer has passed.

Overstimulation

The final issue I want to discuss is overstimulation. Overstimulation is another common issue for someone with ADHD.

When you have ADHD, your brain tends not to regulate emotions as well as sensory input. When it receives too much, it might not tune it out the way an average person would, and it might also be hyper-fixate on the small things.

We discussed that Trinity felt like the toothpaste burned her mouth in one example. Other people might find a shower overstimulating or something like wet hair hanging on their back triggering. Simply put, there are many things that can create this issue.

The best solution is often to sit down with your kiddo and discuss these. Ask them what the hygiene process feels like, if it's too much, and try to dig deeper into why. Not everyone will have the language about overstimulation at hand in their minds and ready to go, so you may have to do some digging or present the topic of overstimulation and what it means before you settle down to discuss it.

Once you and your kiddo narrow down what might be causing the problem, try to look for a solution. If the toothpaste is too minty, get a different one. You can even try kids' toothpaste if it will help, as it's made to do the same thing and often has a fruity flavor. If the feeling of a shower is too much, try a bath. Solutions that minimize or take care of the issue can be discussed if it's something after the fact, like wet hair.

Additional Steps and Tips

Patience Is Key

In this situation, patience is going to be your best friend. It will probably take time to make regular hygiene practices a consistent habit. There will be some great days, some relapses, and days where they just refuse. Don't give in but make it a habit to remain gently firm.

Discuss the Issue

It might be a surface-level thing, like overstimulation or simply trouble sticking to a schedule. These issues have solutions that can make the battle a much easier one for you.

As children become teens, this discussion step is also great for helping them with their desires for independence and being treated like adults.

Accept That Some Things Might Be Out Of Your Control

Your child is a teen now, and they have more agency and autonomy over their body. At this point, you cannot exactly forcibly put them in the shower, and you cannot forcibly brush their teeth. If it is at a point where they are genuinely upset and having a meltdown about the situation, then let it go. It's harming them and you mentally. You can always start the next day.

What you can control is holding them accountable. Verbal reminders, withholding rewards, and if they are younger, making them go back and try again if their work wasn't adequate are all things that can help manage the situation.

Ask the Deeper Questions

First, is there a physical reason they don't want to shower or brush their teeth?

Some children have very sensitive gums, so when they are brushed, they bleed. This might freak them out, and it might be painful.

Is the soap they are using okay? Do they show any signs of being allergic? Does it make their skin itch? Find out.

Next, let's talk about the mental health side of hygiene. First of all, if someone is doing poorly with their mental health, then proper hygiene is often the first thing to go.

We talked a little about depression already. Anxiety can be another factor. If your teen has anxiety tied to certain aspects of hygiene maintenance, then pushing the issue might be hurting them. Talk to them about this, especially if you notice signs of anxiety or panic setting in. A professional can advise on strategies that will help.

Having "Talks"

If your child isn't a fan of hygiene practices and doesn't understand why they are important, they will fight tooth and nail against it.

In order to get them in on your efforts, you may need to sit them down and explain why you are taking these steps.

Explain that basic hygiene needs to be done regularly, or else things tend to build up. Let them know hygiene can prevent sickness and infections, and it helps with body odor and acne.

Try to set up a separate time and space to have this conversation. Having it in the middle of an argument will likely result in your words not being taken seriously.

Sit down at a time that differs from when they are supposed to shower or get ready for bed. Lay out your talking points and be prepared to discuss them in detail.

As your child grows and develops, understanding this will be important. If this is an area your teen struggles with, as many teens do, these steps can help!

Chapter Two
Keeping Them Healthy

Collin's birthday is only a few months away. At 18, he will be leaving in about six months for college. While Collin does well in many ways, his parents have one major concern.

Collin has never cared much about what goes into his body. He rarely feels like cooking, so he will often grab a snack that is less than healthy and sit down to eat it. His mother has tried to talk to him about the dangers of this and how cooked food is often better for him, but Collin brushes off her concerns.

His family is also concerned with the exercise level Collin displays. He will often play video games for a long time, which his parents have accepted as his primary interest, but he rarely goes outside to exercise.

His parents are really looking to set him on the right track, but they are running out of time.

Diet and exercise are important to everyone's health, especially for those with ADHD.

The frontal lobe of the brain of someone who has ADHD is often functioning at a reduced capacity. Diet and exercise, however, can significantly improve a person's brain function. Making sure that one is eating healthy and getting some activity can go a long way in ensuring that they remain healthy and can also improve their functioning.

So, how do we instill these habits before they leave?

The short answer is action-based encouragement. By actively modeling behaviors and encouraging them to get involved, you set them up for success later in life!

Diet

Healthy eating is something that much of the world struggles with, and many of us are just... busy. Like Collin, we gravitate toward ready-made foods because it's easier, and they are already there. We need to work on changing this as much as possible.

Why Is It So Important to Have a Healthy Diet Plan?

First, let's start with the benefits.

By eating a highly varied, natural diet, you are aiding your mind and body.

Physically, by eating a healthy diet, your body will run better, and you will have an easier time getting up, moving around, and enjoying being alive. It's important to note that weight has little bearing on this. People on two opposite ends of the BMI spectrum may function relatively similarly if they both eat healthy diets.

Physically, it will help you live longer as well. A healthy diet has been continuously linked to a longer life span and more enjoyment of that life.

Now mentally, a healthy diet can add clarity to your thoughts. It sharpens your focusing power and can improve your attention span, especially when ADHD is involved. Furthermore, it can have a positive impact on your overall mental health. With the increased brain function, your brain can create chemicals like dopamine more easily.

Now, what can happen if we follow a poor diet in our lifetime?

You might first run into heart disease and its associated conditions. A diet high in things like red meat, saturated fats, and sweets can lead to a heart attack happening much earlier in life.

This is because a lot of the fat and sugar get stuck while they are carried along by the bloodstream. These fat deposits start small, but they can build up over time, leading to high cholesterol levels. Because these deposits are building up, your blood has to work harder to make it through your arteries, leading to high blood pressure. The next thing you have to worry about is a heart attack, as the fat deposits can build to where they close up an artery completely. A heart attack will happen when the blood cannot reach the heart.

The link is less studied, but poor diet has also been associated with various cancers, including lung and liver cancer. Fat deposits in both organs (which is a scary thought in itself) are believed to play a huge role.

Does this mean that you are automatically destined to suffer this fate if you eat steak? Not at all. A diet takes a long time to have this big of an effect on the body. Many people reach their 40s before they start to notice that there's anything wrong, and it doesn't take a toll until they are about 50 or 60. Genetics is also a factor.

You can still eat these foods in moderation as well. You may still have that piece of chocolate cake, just not every single day.

The younger your teen is introduced to this information, the better, but no age is too late.

Use pictures and visuals, like food pyramids and bodily circulatory systems, to break the information down. By making it visual, you are more likely to make this information stick.

Once you discuss the *why* with your teen, it's time to move on to the *how*. After all, this information is great, but it doesn't address a plan on what to do.

Use a Plan Like MyPlate

It's interesting that with the creation of so many fad diets (Paleo, Keto, Whole 30, and intermittent fasting, just to name a few), the healthiest thing for our bodies is still outlined in the government resource known as MyPlate. Unlike fad diets, which can be created by anyone with an internet connection and a small amount of knowledge of the body, MyPlate was created with input from dieticians all across the country. Most countries will have a very similar resource specific to their nation (and their nation's food supply) that people can access, and MyPlate is the American version of this eating plan.

MyPlate and its international cousins are visual. For those with ADHD, a visual of what's going on can help them follow it. For additional guidance, you can write out exactly how much is needed and recommended in each little section on the chart.

So, how much of each group is recommended? For teens who are 14 years of age or more and have a need for about 2000 calories a day, these are the numbers. If your child is a bit younger or their calorie needs are different, then these numbers might vary slightly, and the information can be found on myplate.gov.

For fruits, about two cups a day is recommended. It's stressed that it doesn't really matter what form the fruits are found in; it just matters that it is pure fruit. Fresh fruit is fine, and so is canned or frozen fruit. Fruit juice is good too, so long as it's 100% fruit juice and no additional sugars are added. Fruits add vitamins and minerals to the diet that wouldn't be there otherwise. Some examples include fiber and vitamin C.

Next up are vegetables. It's recommended to have about 2 1/2 cups of vegetables daily, slightly more than a person's fruit intake. These vegetables also add key vitamins and minerals to the diet and help with skin, eyesight, and heart health. Like fruits, you can have them in any form, but what is going to be important is having variety. Different vegetables will help your body do different things.

For example, if your two and a half cups of vegetables only consist of carrots, you are doing a huge favor for your eyesight and immune system. However, you are missing out on other nutrients, such as iron from spinach.

Next up is protein. The recommendation for this is five and a half ounces. This can come from a certain amount of meat; a single egg is considered an ounce. So is about a quarter cup of legumes (non-processed beans). Tofu is also in the protein group. One thing that MyPlate stresses are that these come from lean proteins (meaning that the protein contains less fat). These include chicken and other white meats like turkey, fish, eggs, tofu, and legumes. It primarily excludes red meat such as steak, lamb, and pork. Again, these are okay occasionally, but they shouldn't be a part of the everyday diet.

Next is dairy, where about 3 cups a day are recommended. Dairy includes cow's milk and things like cheese and yogurt. If your kiddo isn't a big milk drinker, do not fear, as there are other ways to get what you're looking for. Just make sure that they enjoy fruits and vegetables high in vitamin D and that they eat food like yogurt or cheese. If your child is lactose intolerant, then fortified soy milk has been enriched to contain the same benefits (just make sure they are fortified).

Finally, the last food group is grains. Many diets, including MyPlate, specify that the grain should be whole wheat or at least enriched. The reason for this is because grains from white items (white bread, white rice, noodles) have all been stripped of the vitamins and minerals they should contain. White products are generally easier to work with. Enriched items have had the necessities added back in, but they are still highly processed. Look out for products like whole wheat bread, noodles, and brown rice. MyPlate recommends that about six ounces of grains be consumed per day. For reference, about one slice of bread is one ounce.

MyPlate, as I stated above, is the diet that meets the needs of nearly everyone unless there are specific issues that need to be addressed. Many other diets may do long-term harm. For example, keto has been linked to heart disease because of the extremely high protein intake.

If your teen would like to explore options that aren't related to MyPlate, here are a few cultural diets that they can try.

These diets have gained in popularity because the people in the regions that enjoy them have significantly lower rates of diet-related disease.

The Mediterranean Diet

The Mediterranean diet is native to the countries in Europe that surround the Mediterranean Sea, and this includes Spain, Greece, and Italy.

Interest in this diet plan began when people realized that, unlike the rest of the world, people in this area weren't suffering from heart disease, food-related cancers, or other sicknesses that have now been related to the consumption of certain types of food. Research in this area told people that their diet was the reason. They eat the exact same food we do, but there are certain things they do differently.

Organic foods in many countries tend to be very expensive, and they are sold in smaller quantities than food that has been chemically treated or genetically modified. This isn't the case in the Mediterranean region. Thanks to the sea and the climate, it's easier to grow fresh fruits and vegetables in this area, so many of their products are organic.

The way their diet is structured differs a lot as well. The main part of the diet is fruits and vegetables, and these are consumed with every meal and often (but not always) make up the main portion of the meal.

Next up are nuts and seeds, which the region has heavy access to and can add to almost anything.

Legumes and potatoes follow as next on the list. Legumes, which refer to non-processed beans like black beans, red kidney beans, lima beans, and many others, are a great source of protein, and these are a great way to have protein for those looking to eat less meat.

Fresh potatoes can be prepared in a variety of different ways, and they are a good source of carbs and very filling.

Speaking of carbs, the next thing that makes up a massive part of their diet is whole grains. The white grains that we discussed in the section above don't really have a place in the Mediterranean diet. Instead, things like bread, pasta, rice, and other foods created by grains are made with whole grains.

Next on the list are herbs and spices. We all like adding flavor to our food, and the Mediterranean diet makes plenty of room for this. Fresh herbs are a part of many recipes, and for those who still want more, you can just add a little spice.

You may have noticed that we've talked about meat very little so far. Unlike diets found in regions like America, meat isn't a massive part of every meal. The exception might be fish and shellfish. Thanks to the Mediterranean Sea, this region has a vast amount of seafood available. It's usually fresh as well since people may fish for it themselves, or it's bought quickly after the catch. Fish consumption may not be in every meal, but it is often a part of one's daily diet.

Olive oil is the final major component of the Mediterranean diet. Most cooking is done with lightly processed olive oil. It tends to be the healthiest oil to use, and it gives food a great flavor.

White meats, dairy, and eggs aren't consumed as often, but they are a part of the Mediterranean diet. Researchers say they are consumed anywhere from two times a week to once a day.

Finally, red meats and sweets don't play much of a role in the Mediterranean diet. They are consumed maybe once or twice a week. With fish being so plentiful and fresh fruit within reach, there is often no need to consume a lot of these.

Not only is the Mediterranean diet good for avoiding disease, but it can also improve brain health.

This diet isn't just about the foods you eat. It comes down to what you eat and how you eat it as well. Recipes for Mediterranean meals are a little different, but the food for it tastes fantastic.

If your child has trouble with MyPlate or wants to try something different, then this is a great alternative.

Asian Diet

Traditional Asian diets have also been explored as the rate of disease related to food consumption is very low. The foods traditionally found in Asian cultures are slightly more processed but not nearly as much as those that are found in other regions.

One thing that stands out and sets it apart from the Mediterranean diet is the large use of white rice. Not only does rice exist for use as, well, rice, but it's also used to create several products. There are rice noodles and rice paper, just to name a few. One way or another, you are bound to find rice in your diet by following their eating plan!

Grains of all types end up being a massive part of the diet as well. There's wheat, barley, corn, and more. Grains and rice make up the base of most Asian meals.

Next up are fruits, vegetables, nuts, seeds, and legumes. These also make up a massive part of the diet, and they are consumed with at least two out of three meals each day. Vegetable-based oils are their primary cooking oil as well.

Seafood is consumed with at least one meal a day. Since many Asian countries find that they either border the ocean or at the very least they have several rivers and water sources, they have plenty of fish. Like the Mediterranean region, it's easy to get a hold of when it's fresh, so it's a bigger part of their diet.

Dairy plays a bigger role in the Asian diet. With many milk products available, it's consumed on an almost daily basis.

White meats, eggs, and sweets are consumed once or twice a week. Red meat is consumed monthly at most.

Like the Mediterranean diet, the Asian diet has unique ways of cooking that differ from other regions of the world. It's absolutely worth checking out, even if you are just looking to try new things with your child.

A great perk about trying a healthy, culturally based diet is that you can engage your child's creativity. Letting them try things, learn different ways to cook, and discover new balances in how they eat can all add interest to eating healthy.

A massive part of cultural diets is also the exercise that goes into them. The Mediterranean lifestyle involves a lot of walking and biking. Asian lifestyles put a lot of emphasis on a zen-based exercise like yoga. Children often learn it from a young age.

Since exercise is also a huge part of health, we are going to talk about it next.

Exercise

Remember our previous story? Collin's parents are struggling to get him outside to exercise, and it worries them. They decide they are going to sit down with Collin and talk about the why.

Why Should We Engage In Exercise?

One of the most basic reasons exercise holds value is that it can be a social experience. If you attend a class, or just plan to do it with friends, or you engage in sports, you can find that a lot of people are there for the same reason you are, and you can connect with them.

Another reason to engage in regular exercise is that it can help you sleep better. Sleep has always been an essential part of regenerating our bodies. That being said, it seems that today, we always have so much to worry about that sleeping falls to the wayside. We are often too busy, or our minds can't stop spinning long enough for us to get some real rest. Exercise can help us out with the second one. It tires out the body, and the time spent is very therapeutic for your brain as well.

If you have been feeling drained lately, then exercise can help you with that too! Exercise gets your heart rate up, and by giving your mind a chance to get away from work, your head might be clearer. Something as simple as a morning walk can add a lot of energy to your day!

When it comes to conditions associated with ADHD, we often have to talk about depression and low self-esteem. Both are common issues that sufferers face. Regular exercise, even if it involves simply going for a walk, can help. Exercise sends off chemicals like serotonin and dopamine, which are motivation and mood-boosting chemicals. Exercising outside, in the sunlight, also impacts how we see things. It allows us a break, giving our minds a chance to relax. Finally, exercising is an act of taking care of our body. This alone makes us feel better and more confident in our bodies, even if nothing changes.

If you ever feel like doctors are pushing you to exercise, there is a good reason for it! Exercise is a preventative factor in staving off disease. Your body, and as a result, your immune system, will tend to be stronger. Exercise also encourages stronger blood flow and improves muscle tension. With exercise, decreased rates of heart disease, high blood sugar, high cholesterol levels, and other heart health-related conditions are all seen the more a person exercises. Another thing that sees a decrease is the risk of diabetes. Strokes are less common in those who regularly exercise as well. Additionally, exercise involves continuous movement, which can prevent problems like arthritis later in life. Because your body is naturally stronger in life, it can prevent falls from being detrimental.

Finally, the most obvious reason that many of us exercise is for weight control. Weight isn't everything when it comes to our health, but it is one factor that can be used to measure it. Exercise can help us at least keep a consistent weight and maybe even help us shed a few pounds.

With these reasons in hand, it's time to talk to your kiddo. When we talk about building up a habit of exercise for later in life, give them reasons why. If there is something on the list that they are struggling with or that they are particularly worried about in the future, then connect exercise to that. The exception to this is weight. Exercise can help, but if that is your teen's concern and they don't see the scale move, they might get discouraged.

How To Encourage Exercise

In addition to talking about the "why," illustrating the "how" can also be important. Here are a few ways.

Memberships to Gyms or Groups.

A gym membership, where they can go and work out, can help them at least have a place to go where there is equipment. They can use this to their heart's content. This can be especially helpful if your teen has a car. On rougher days when they need to get some energy out, they have a healthy place to do so. Some gyms offer classes in things like dance, weightlifting, and yoga. If your teen wants to try some of these out, then they can!

Make It Family Time

If exercise becomes a family activity, then that becomes additional encouragement. Your teen will feel less alone in their efforts, and as a family, you have more time to connect. Walks around the neighborhood or a game of ball or frisbee are some great examples of simple things you can do.

Video Game Exercise

Let's go back to Collin for a moment. He loves video games. He has a couple of different gaming systems. In their research, his parents came across some ideas that could help Collin.

Today there are a few gaming systems that come with an active component. The two most common are the Xbox and the Wii. Both systems have games that are designed around the idea of exercise. Many of us enjoy our screen time, and it is very possible to enjoy it actively.

Sports

One final great way to get your child into the habit of regularly exercising is to get them into a sport that they like. There is basketball, baseball, dance, soccer, swimming, and so many more out there. Sports absolutely allow for exercise. They also include a major social component. When you do these things with friends, you are much more likely to enjoy them.

These strategies illustrate some of the ways you can get your teen into a pattern of activity. Which one works best will depend on the person. When you sit down with your teen to talk about why it's important, it's also going to help if you address how this is going to be done.

What do they want to do? Is there a sport they want to try? Do they want to go to the gym? Do they want to spend more time as a family? If there is something they are leaning towards, try it. If it's something they already have an interest in, they are more likely to be invested in it.

Cooking

It's time to circle back to food, as it's a vital component of being healthy. Eating healthy and exercising are just two components of being a healthy person. Cooking is important, as it ties everything together very well.

Cooking is going to be a huge part of eating right. In order to have good, healthy food, you must know how to make it. The activity of cooking food for oneself can have similar benefits to exercise. Teaching children and teens how to cook can be fun... or it could be a disaster. Next, we're going to discuss some ways to get your teen engaged in the process.

Tips For Creating Enthusiasm For Cooking

Get Their Thoughts and Opinions About What You Are Cooking

Introduce them to the process and ingredients behind meals that they and other members of the family enjoy. You can also look at trying new things and getting their help with it.

If you are looking to try something new, find a few recipes that sound really good, and ask your teen to look over them and choose one. You can get their help with picking ingredients up at the store too.

Being involved in the cooking process can stir curiosity, and it also makes a person more comfortable with the process.

Engage Your Minds Senses

We have five senses through which we explore the world. Cooking is very capable of engaging them all. When getting your ADHD teen interested in cooking or food, try engaging as many senses as you possibly can.

What do they see? This one seems pretty straightforward at first, but to get them more involved with this sense, add some color to the dish. Colored vegetables are the most popular way to do this.

Next, what can they touch? What textures are on the plate? What's the feeling of a well-cooked steak? What is the sauce like? There might be some sanitary concerns with this step, so you can limit it to their plate or have them describe what the textures would feel like to them.

The sound of cooking may not seem like it has much involvement in cooking until you are frying some vegetables or cooking meat on the grill. You can hear the sounds of sizzling as you cook food. You can hear the knife slide through different vegetables. All of these things can appeal to our sense of hearing.

The sense of smell is an important one in a kitchen, and asking your teen to stop and step into the kitchen with their eyes closed, ready to pick up that scent, can be a great way to get them excited to cook. It's also important for everyone to know what burning food smells like so they can react quickly.

The final sense is, of course, taste. Have them taste everything. Have them try the food before and after you cook it (when it's safe to do so) so that they can taste the difference. Have them try a variety of new things and introduce them to new spices.

The brain of someone with ADHD seeks thrilling experiences. By recreating this and engaging their senses, you have a good way to create such an experience for them.

Add Some New Elements To Their Safe Foods

People with ADHD and other brain-diverse conditions tend to have certain safe foods that they are willing to eat, especially on hard days. Now, this step might not be such a good idea on one of those hard days, but on days where they are especially engaged in learning, or if they are really unsure about the cooking process, try this.

If one of their comfort foods is mac and cheese, then try to add some things to it, like meat chunks and vegetables, to make it a balanced meal. Try different brands of mac and cheese too, as some are healthier than others.

Let's say that their comfort food is toast. Toast can be dressed up in so many different ways. Add a nut spread like peanut butter or Nutella. Add an avocado, an egg, or even both. These are just a few examples.

For those that are really hesitant about trying new things, these can help bring them out of their shell one step at a time.

Experimenting Can Be Messy

When it comes to ADHD, we all know that things are rarely clean. What we do see is a lot of mess or organized chaos. If getting them into the kitchen means that there is a mess involved, then so be it. Exploration, especially with food, can do that.

Don't worry; chapter six spends time on cleaning skills.

Mix Foods That Your Child Doesn't Like With Ones That They Do.

We can create a lot of stress for ourselves by trying to get our teens to eat things they don't want. It might come down to a blanket refusal.

This is tricky because they can't avoid certain foods, especially vegetables, forever. So, how do we help with this?

First, remember that we aren't really dealing with children but rather with teens. If we try to be sneaky about adding foods they don't like into their meals, they will notice pretty quickly. Have a conversation with them about the importance and mention that this is a strategy you are going to try. Maybe it's adding some new vegetables into a casserole they like or another way to get them. Ask your teen if they have any suggestions as well because having their input can mean that they are more willing to try the dish.

Flavors

New flavors mean new and thrilling experiences for your ADHD teen. Herbs can add a ton of flavor to a dish, and they are often very healthy. The same is mostly true for spices. Let your teen try them separately and in cooking and have them pick out a few that they really like. You can use this in other dishes later.

Let Them Lead

Most of what we talked about so far has been about introducing them to new foods, senses, and tastes, but most of this is led by you. You aren't going to be there to lead them in cooking when they are older, so at some point, it is important to hand the reins over.

Ask them to make a meal every week and let them have control over it. If you are worried about injury potential, stay close by but gradually withdraw from this the more you see that they are getting it right.

As you go through the steps above, they might have some spices that they want to try, or they may have already thought of some ways to spice up their comfort meal. When we are trying to get them into the kitchen, anything that they can do by themselves is a huge step in the right direction.

Invest In Some Cooking Items That They Might Be Interested In

Cooking stores tend to have a lot of random tools that have a specific purpose. While they might not interest us, your teen might become very invested in them! If there are some tools that seem to pique their interest, get them.

Even in the case of general tools for cooking, a new pan or spatula can be exciting.

Be a Role Model

This last part is one of the most important. If your teen sees you as always cooking and eating healthier and well-balanced meals, they are naturally more likely to join that effort.

Tips For Those Who Are Starting To Cook

Think of a famous chef you know! Gordon Ramsey? Martha Stewart? Do you think that they naturally learned how to cook like that, or was it a process?

It's often a process. Some parts of cooking are going to be straightforward, but there are many mistakes that can be made when your teen is starting out, especially when they have ADHD. The tips I have here for you are great for beginners, but, also, they can really be great for anyone.

Reread the Recipe and Keep It Handy

Today, we can find a lot of the recipes we have just by using our phones. The trouble is that it can be hard to then keep track of where the recipe goes. You are going to need that, especially as you start. Today, most phones come with a bookmark feature. You can use it to create a separate reading list for yourself that includes all of your recipes. Most of them give you a chance to name the bookmark so that you can name it something like the name of the dish rather than keeping the webpage name (which can be really hard to look for).

Another thing to make sure you do before you start the cooking process is to read the recipe all the way through and then reread it. Make sure you know what each step is going to be before you begin. That way, you only have to glance at it during your preparation.

Egg Tip: Ice Or Vinegar

Hard-boiled eggs are relatively easy to cook. They are very difficult to peel, though, unless you try a method to make it easier. One of my favorite methods is putting the eggs in an ice bath immediately after you take them out. By doing this, the egg itself is less attached to the shell and will peel easier. Another common method is adding vinegar to the boiling water.

Finally, how long you let the eggs boil depends on what exactly you are trying to do! If you want softer, gooier eggs, then you can leave them in for as little as four minutes.

Freezing Your Foods

A lot of people today will prepare meals and freeze things for later. If you and your teen are busy, setting time aside at the beginning of the week to cook together and then having these meals ready can be a lifesaver. It does introduce another element: freezing things.

I love fresh fruits and vegetables as much as the next person, but I cannot deny that they tend to go bad before my daughter and I can eat them. Cutting things up and then freezing them for later has been one way we can combat this problem. It helps to do some of the basic parts of preparing them to eat first (cutting the tops off strawberries, slicing carrots, etc.), and then freezing them will make it so that you can just take what you need at the beginning of the day.

Try to seal and get as much air out of the bags as possible when you do this. If the fruit or vegetable is sensitive to spoiling, then having the air in the bag can still cause it to go brown, even if it's frozen.

Another thing you can do if you want to avoid freezer burn is to add cooking oil to the items. This works better with vegetables, but a light coating of something like olive oil can make a difference in how well they do in the freezer. It usually won't affect the taste of the food.

Take Care Of Your Knives

Knife care isn't something that everyone considers to be a part of their cooking routine, but it should be.

Most cooking excerpts will recommend that you sharpen your knives at least once a week (or more, depending on how often they are used). The idea of giving your teen sharper knives when they are just starting out in their cooking journey might seem daunting at first, but there is a good reason for it! They are actually safer than dull knives.

With sharp knives, you get a clean, even slice. Dull knives have a harder time cutting through things, and they will slip a lot more easily and often onto someone's finger (we've all been there). Even if you do manage to cut yourself with a sharp knife, you are likely to realize it sooner!

Experiment With Spice Mixes

Traditional spices always add something unique to food. Spice blends are common, especially in foods from other cultures. If you and your teen are getting bored with the same recipes, don't be afraid to try a spice blend. You can pick one up from a store, but it's more fun to create your own. There are online sources that have lists of what spices are used in different cultures. You can check this out and try some different mixes!

Group Like Steps Together

Here is another great reason to read the recipe first before you do anything else.

A recipe will often have you prepare one part of the meal and then the next. This has you in a cycle of preparing, then cooking, then back to preparing, and then cooking again until you finally combine the ingredients all into a dish. This process can be annoying. It's hard to be efficient.

Grouping your like steps together can cut down on the time you actually spend cooking.

Prepare everything first. If there is something that needs chopped or mixed, get that out of the way so that you can turn to the actual cooking part.

Then, cook everything. A lot of the time, you can reduce the time you spend cooking by half.

Being able to impart some tips that make cooking easier can help you, and your teen start learning how to cook. The next thing I want to share with you is some basic skills to start your teen with!

Basic Skills To Start With When Cooking

Cutting and Chopping

If you've grown up in or around the kitchen, then certain cuts and other things are going to be very familiar to you. For example, what is the difference between chopped and minced food? Also, how do you hold a knife to get what you want out of it?

These skills are important to the success of most recipes.

Degrees of Cooking

How do you like your steak? Do you prefer your bacon crispy? Do you like soft vegetables, or do you prefer them to have a crunch still after they are cooked? Do you like burnt bits of food, or is that not your thing?

How often have you considered questions like this when you are teaching your teen?

Cooking something isn't as simple as it seems. Most foods have to be cooked to a certain point for safety reasons, but after that, it's up to you. Spend some time on this part of cooking, and see if you can find out to which degree your child likes things.

Boiling

It's been a minute since I've left college, but one thing I remember is that a lot of my peers weren't sure of another basic part of cooking: boiling water. Make sure to go over this at least once with your teen and discuss some of the basic foods they can make, including noodles, macaroni and cheese, and hard-boiled eggs.

Cleanliness

I want to highlight this because many people with ADHD understandably struggle with this. In a kitchen, a lack of cleanliness can make you sick. So can cross-contamination. These are absolutely important to teach.

First, there is the concept of basic cleanliness in a kitchen. Teach your child about it. Let them know that by keeping up with cleaning in the kitchen, it keeps away bugs and bacteria.

Cross-contamination is also something you want to talk about. Many of us aren't aware when it happens, but it can make people very sick. Imagine having your teen cook chicken and make a salad for dinner. They cut and start cooking the chicken first because it will take longer, and they can kind of just keep an eye on it while they cut the vegetables.

Not knowing cross-contamination procedures, they immediately switch to chopping vegetables, using the same knife and cutting board without any cleaning procedures done in between. The entire salad has had contact with raw chicken and is now a petri dish of bacteria. Everyone who eats that salad is bound to get sick, and the teen won't realize their mistake until later.

Making sure that your teen knows about cross-contamination in advance can prevent this exact scenario from happening.

Basic Dishes

What are some basic things you can teach your teen to make?

Pasta is one option. Making noodles and throwing on some sauce of their choice creates a great meal.

Another thing is eggs. It's easy to make for breakfast, and you don't have to do a lot of steps.

Sandwiches can be made. And so can many other things. Start by teaching these dishes so that even if cooking isn't their biggest interest, they still have something to take away, and they also have something they can build and grow on.

Food and exercise are so important to our physical health. Our mental health is important too. How do we take care of that?

Chapter Three
Keeping On Top Of Those Emotions

The parents of fourteen-year-old Riley always tried their best with their daughter. She was their joy in life until she had to deal with life's tougher emotions. Riley was prone to outbursts in the form of yelling until she was purple in the face. She would also have explosive panic attacks, and whenever she got stressed, it was always to a point where she would seem to get physically sick. She was finally diagnosed with ADHD, but that just left her parents with more questions than answers. How did something that was about paying attention relate to what she was experiencing now?

They weren't sure what to do. Riley was relying on them to help, and they weren't sure how to provide it or where to start.

If your teen struggles with their emotions, you've probably been in the position of Riley's parents. Children never mean to lose control, but they do. They rely on us to teach them the right ways of handling things so that they can master their feelings. This is true, even when they have ADHD.

Why Does This Happen?

Let's talk a bit about how ADHD affects the brain. Scientists have theories, but they aren't sure about the cause of ADHD. They also aren't 100 percent sure about what exactly in the brain is going wrong, but several cross-examinations and brain scans have led them to some theories.

The leading theory is that the prefrontal cortex in someone with ADHD grows more slowly on average.

The prefrontal cortex is responsible for language, logic, self-control, attention span, and to some extent, emotions.

ADHD is also believed to inhibit one's dopamine flow. Dopamine is a motivational chemical. Without any dopamine in your system, you don't have the motivation to move, even if danger is lurking nearby.

A final impairment that is important to discuss, especially for this chapter, is the concept of flooding. When a typical brain experiences emotions, they experience them like normal, and then the brain switches off. There are remnants of the chemical that created the emotion, but those will soon fade.

An ADHD brain will heavily struggle to have that regulation. It won't turn on and off as we should expect. Instead, the emotional signals keep going until the brain is overwhelmed with the emotional response. This is called flooding, and it's what leads to outbursts, panic attacks, and other intense displays of emotion.

The chemical wires are what's causing meltdowns like Riley's. Once they got ahold of this information, Riley's parents sat down and explained it to her. She felt relieved to understand what was really going on in her brain. This knowledge alone was able to guide her through some of the more mild attacks she'd experienced.

If you notice that your teen does struggle in this area, then give them this knowledge. Knowing what's going on can help them have more control, as logic can help with emotions, and it can help them understand that they aren't bad people; their brain is just being mean.

There are some emotions that our brain does more than others. Unfortunately, these emotions are the ones that even typically brained adults can struggle with.

Stress

Imagine living with ADHD and having to deal with all of the functions it impairs. You're struggling to pay attention at school and work. You're struggling to make sense of what's going on around you. You're struggling with cleaning and maintenance. Everything you're expected to do feels overwhelming to you. It can lead to a huge stress response buildup.

Let's put ourselves in Riley's shoes. She's often very stressed. She has trouble waking up to her alarm. Her room is often messy, so it's hard to gather everything. In class, she has a lot of trouble paying attention, and the teachers like to call on her in order to call her out for this. She has an incredibly difficult time concentrating on homework, and then her parents stress that her room is cleaned and she helps with chores.

For an average person, all of this makes sense, and it's a part of life. For a person with ADHD, as they struggle to do one task after another, it creates stress that they can't escape. Riley's parents get worried because an extra chore or an extra assignment that Riley forgot about can send her over the edge.

Anxiety

Stress is a feeling that is the result of an event. There is a direct cause and effect relationship with stress, but not with anxiety. You can have anxiety about something that has happened, something that might happen, or something that will never happen. There isn't a direct link between the issues at play here.

Stress can cause anxiety, though, and Riley's parents notice it. She tends to get very worked up very quickly. Even in moments when they are watching TV as a family, Riley can't seem to calm down. They've noticed many little habits that Riley seems to have picked up, and it worries them.

Anger

Anger is an emotion that everyone has the right to feel. However, we must be careful in how we express it. Riley has received four detentions in total because she got angry and went off at a teacher. This is very uncharacteristic of their child, who is normally very sweet and well-tempered.

Riley has also gone off on them multiple times. Physically, she will only throw herself to the ground or physically hit her head against the wall, but her parents have heard horror stories about children who broke walls or whose parents had to press charges.

Anger is one of the biggest emotions that flood the system of an ADHD person. It will keep going until they fly into a rage. Even as Riley has calmed down in the past, she still has felt overwhelmingly angry. She just didn't have the energy to continue the outburst.

In order for our children to be successful, they need to be able to control these emotions. Give them a chance to work through it if you can. Help them through different strategies so that they can hopefully do it on their own soon.

Strategies For Dealing With These Emotions

Stress

If we have just the right amount of stress, then we are motivated to focus and get our work done. But, when we get to the point where we have too much stress, the situation starts to get out of control. When you have ADHD, and your brain is capable of flooding, then it becomes harder to walk that line.

If your teen keeps trying to get their work done but finds that they keep struggling to, suggest things like listening to music. Have them create a to-do list or keep a planner. Having one of these makes it easier to make sure that things are getting done. Fewer things slip through the cracks, you don't have to do the tracking with your brain, and it's satisfying to cross something off after it has been completed.

Another thing that can help is to only focus on one thing and get that done before moving on. Trying to do multiple tasks at once isn't going to help. That may actually hurt you since the time it takes to switch between tasks is going to take up more time than it would to focus on one task. The exception to this is when you are stuck and can't move forward.

For example, if your teen is struggling with their math homework and no matter what they do, they just can't figure it out and seem to be close to tears, then it might be time to move on to another subject. Going back to their math homework with a fresh pair of eyes can make a difference in their interpretation.

Another thing to do is make sure to focus on one task at a time. Teens often get a ton of homework, and it can be overwhelming to think about how much you might have to do. Looking at one piece at a time instead of the big picture can help you focus on what needs to be done without getting stressed.

Another tip is taking breaks. Make sure that this is a part of your teen's routine if they have several hours of homework to do. Have them take a five-minute breathing break after they get through a subject. Have them get through a few subjects and then go and exercise. Things like this can help the stress response relax and prevent flooding.

Teach your teen to speak up for themself and offer them a safe space to do that. If they feel like they can't tell others when they are overwhelmed, then they won't. Eventually, their silence will lead to a meltdown.

Communication is key. Speaking up when they need to is part of it. Another part is just ensuring that communication is something your child is good at, and they should be able to communicate with you about what they need from you. They should be able to communicate with their teachers if there is something that they are struggling with. Being able to speak your needs can help to reduce stress significantly.

Problem-solving abilities are going to be another preventative factor in stress management. By being able to sit there and figure out the answer to the problem at hand, your teen is going to find themselves less stressed. For example, the problem could easily be that there is an overwhelming amount of homework for the weekend. Your teen may solve a problem that involves tackling his math homework Friday night, his English and history papers on Saturday, and his science on Sunday. Everything gets done with a solution that your teen was able to think through.

When all of these don't work, have some things ready that just naturally reduce stress. Get your favorite snack. Meditate (which we will talk about more later in this chapter).

If there is something that doesn't have to be dealt with, then don't. It's not imperative that they do the extra credit if there are other assignments. If they have a free period before math class and know that they can get it done, move on.

Finally, give them as much control as possible in their lives. They are going to be an adult soon, so being able to have control over their life while they still have your guidance close by is going to give them a chance to experiment safely. Let them choose their classes and electives, so long as they are meeting graduation requirements.

On a day-to-day basis, let them choose where they want to do their homework. It could be inside, outside, in their room, or at the kitchen table. Letting them have the option of sitting wherever they like can alleviate some of the stress they might face.

Stress often has a direct cause, so many of its strategies are aimed at reducing the magnitude of the cost so that the person can better deal with it later. Our next topic is anxiety, which is a bit different.

Anxiety

As we talked about earlier, anxiety isn't directly related to a cause, so managing the cause might not help how a person is feeling—because of this, trying to work on the direct cause might make it worse because your teen is focusing on the problem even more.

Sadly, we can't avoid most causes of anxiety. Things like going to school are common triggers. What we can do is work on the thoughts and feelings surrounding anxiety.

Create a brainstorm for anxiety and its causes. Talk to your teen about the specifics of their anxiety and see what can be done to ease it. Let's continue to use school as an example.

Your teen has anxiety about going to school. When does it start? Where are they? They might answer that it starts as soon as they get up, when they start the commute to school, or when they first walk into the building. Ask them if there are any specific triggers. Is it the tone of voice of a teacher or seeing certain people? Have these people done anything to warrant the anxiety (in which case, what steps can be taken to make sure it doesn't happen again)? Is it just there? What about certain activities or classes at school?

School is a broad thing to be anxious about, but if you and your teen can narrow down the specific reason it's happening, it can make the rest of school more bearable, and it can put more focus on a solution, which is the thing to ask about next.

What happens when they get to school, and they run into the trigger, or the feeling starts to rise? What are some things they can do?

Having a thought-out strategy can ease some of those feelings. Our thoughts are much easier to control, and if we get a good handle on them, it can ease our feelings.

If that doesn't seem to be working, ask your teen about potential distractors. Can they listen to music, doodle, read, or find a simple game that they like that can help?

Logic won't always work on anxiety, but redirections and distractions can have a powerful effect. A final thing for your teens to remember is that, much like ADHD, anxiety can feel like it's a part of your personality. It's not. Yes, you might struggle with it, and it can have a big impact on your everyday life, but that doesn't mean that it's who you are.

It can be tempting for you to step in when their anxiety is high and just fix everything for them. With anxiety being such a toxic emotion, this instinct is natural. Sadly, it will do more harm than good to do this. By stepping in and taking them away from the anxiousness, they are losing a chance to deal with their own problems. Never facing the issues giving them anxiety can make their anxiety worse in the long run. People who suffer from anxiety often find that it never quite leaves them, but they do find ways to manage it the more they interact with it. For your soon-to-be adult, this skill is necessary.

Instead, create a safe space. Provide relief for the anxiety in other ways by letting them come to a place where they don't have to feel it. Give them an opportunity to cool down and breathe. When they are struggling, be someone with who they can talk about their struggles. You don't have to have answers for them, but by being there and being a safe person, their body and mind will give them a break.

One thing to keep in mind is that not every teen will see their home as their safe space. This isn't always because of a lack of sameness in the home. It's often because there is just another area that is familiar and safe to them. It could be a library or a coffee shop. It could be a park or a skating rink. It could be the beach or a pool. Whatever the case might be, that's a safe place. Make time as often as possible for them to visit it, especially after they have to deal with high anxiety situations.

When your teen feels like their anxiety has locked them into a box of sorts and they can't move forward, talk to them about small, incremental goals that they can do that can slowly help them be able to function. It could be that they are terrified to do their homework because they think they are going to fail. A goal for this might be to forget about doing it well. Just finish the assignments and turn them in. Any grade is better than a zero.

In these cases, they also try to steer their mind in a different direction. They already know what's going to happen if their anxieties come true. They've likely spent hours agonizing over it. Ask them what's going to happen if the good outcome is met? What if your kid gets a good grade? Ask them to describe what would happen then.

You might notice a theme that, in dealing with anxiety, there isn't much problem-solving. Instead, it's made to be more about managing feelings. Anxiety is a feeling that needs to be managed, and solving problems won't do the trick. Instead, we focus on how to bring our anxiety levels back down so that we can effectively live life. That's how working with anxiety goes. We can't defeat it as we can with stress, so we instead learn to overcome it.

Anger

It's not uncommon for children with ADHD to have anger issues. Many children with ADHD are in trouble because their anger leads them to act out. As children, trouble looks like a note home to the parents, detention, or suspension.

As adults, losing control of our anger can mean the loss of a job, a loved one, and even criminal charges. Anger cannot go unchecked. It's an emotion that we must deal with and respond appropriately to.

As our children enter their teen years, they have to deal with hormones on top of the flooding that their brain might already experience, creating the perfect conditions for a full tornado of rage.

It's important for teens to have strategies that manage this anger so that they can still live and not have to worry about blowing up at someone.

One such strategy is exercise. A lot of strong emotions can fuel a workout or be channeled into sports. Exercising can help by putting that rage into physical use. Making sufficient time for exercise can help the brain be more at ease as well, instead of keeping these feelings all pent up.

Coach your teen not only by making exercise a regular habit but also by understanding that if they need to take a break during something and walk off some of that energy, they should be able to do so. It is better to take that breather than to go into a rage. Conditions like ADHD are covered by ADA laws, and you can get a doctor to put this in a 504 plan. This means that even if they are at school or work, they should be able to walk away when they need to, and there shouldn't be any consequences (so long as this isn't abused).

Another thing to do is to help your teen work on vocalizing their feelings instead of acting on them. When they start to run into overwhelming anger, which is often due to flooding, work on statements such as "I'm getting very angry right now" or "this anger is too much for me, and I need to step out." The vocalization alone can sometimes help, and it gives the people around them a heads up.

Another thing to do is look into the use of electronics. This one is hard because electronics are such a huge part of our lives, and at this point, your teen probably needs them to complete daily functions. That being said, they've been tied to angry outbursts, as well as other emotional issues such as depression. Try to have your teen spend a certain amount of time away from a screen. This can be reading a book, cooking, eating, or doing something outside. The break can have a powerful effect on the mind, and it can help calm any brewing outbursts.

Another thing to do is to make sure that your child is in touch with their feelings. How can they know that they need to step out and take a walk or that they need to vocalize their feelings if they can't really feel what's about to happen until it's too late? If they are able to identify their emotions as a signal ahead of time, then they can dive into reduction tactics.

Keep in mind, as you prepare your teen for the adult world, that there are some situations that are causing anger that they won't have to deal with. A curfew is one example. When there are issues like these, and they are causing anger, then it's time to sit down and discuss the issue. Try to compromise and let them have a chance to talk about what's going on. If there isn't a need for an issue, but they are getting angry over it, then it may be a good idea to let it go. Your teen will soon find out on their own why it's important to go to bed at a certain time. The misbehavior due to these issues is more attributable to ADHD than anything that they are intentionally doing.

Have your teen keep a record of their emotions and anything they have done that helps them get through negative emotions. This gives them some responsibility for their emotions and how to calm them down.

The final thing that you can do for anger is just to make sure that your teen has a space to talk through it. Anger is an emotion that shouldn't be acted on, as it can destroy great things. It is an emotion that we need to deal with, and discussion can be a huge part of that.

Emotions are tough. Adults with a typical brain will struggle with keeping their emotions in check.

Imagine having ADHD and having to deal with flooding when it comes to stress, anxiety, or anger. It's a difficult thing that is going to require some extra strategies to deal with. At the end of the day, remind your teen that they are not their emotions and that it's going to be challenging, but they have strategies to get through it!

The same is going to be true for our next chapter. Time management is something that everyone struggles with, but this is often more the case for those with ADHD. What additional strategies can help them?

Chapter Four
Time Management and Organization Skills

Let's take a moment to consider the stereotypical ADHD adult. They wake up late because they "forgot" to set their alarm. They rush around, and everything around them is a mess. They can't find anything, and there is chaos and clutter everywhere.

They leave the house looking like a cluttered mess and forget half the things they were supposed to bring with them.

While they work, they are constantly distracted by other things. They seem to always be focused on other things, and they aren't as competent. There is no organization in their life; they are always late and have terrible time management. A company cannot discriminate by not hiring someone with ADHD, but because of these stereotypes, they may try to avoid it at all costs.

It's easy for someone with ADHD to fall into this stereotype, but there are so many strategies that help prevent it, so how do we help your teen?

The younger you can start these strategies, the more ingrained the habits will be.

Time Management

There are so many things that we need to get done each day. Those things don't often include timed obligations such as appointments, work schedules, and the need to be in class on time.

The ADHD brain doesn't naturally keep a schedule, so it's essential to make use of helpful outside resources to do this.

Have Something Near You At All Times That Can Give You the Time

This one is kind of easy as we all seem to have our phones on us constantly. That is perfect if that can give your teen the time at all hours. But they might not always have it on them, not make a habit of glancing at it, or they might not be allowed to look at it (many high schools still ban the use of phones in school).

Watches are another great alternative. Having a clock in their room can be beneficial for them as well. Having time constantly near them can help them with punctuality, and it can also provide a way to time tasks. If your child has a day where they aren't really interested in doing anything, then setting appropriate timers for tasks can help. Conversely, if they have a day where they are hyper-focused on something, but you are worried that it will absorb too much of their day, then you can have them set timers for that too.

If, even with a clock, your teen still struggles with punctuality, have them set alarms for each step of the day. At 6 a.m., they get up and make their bed. At 6:15, they have breakfast. At 6:45, they get dressed and ready for the day. This pattern continues until they have their alarm for when it's time to leave. If you worry that they will still be late, try adding five to ten additional minutes into their routine somewhere. It could be that they get up ten minutes earlier than they need to or that you think of the event you're trying to go to as being ten minutes earlier than it is scheduled (and you write it down as such). This way, there is a little bit of lax time for them to play with, and they have a good chance of getting there on time.

Create A Timesheet

It can be easy for anyone to forget all of the little details in a day, especially when a person has ADHD.

Think of a school schedule and all the activities and homework following it. Things are bound to slip through the cracks, especially if it's the start of a semester and the schedule is new.

Writing out a timesheet can be helpful for your teen. They can try a simple one that tells them where their classes are and where they need to be, or they can make it highly detailed. Some timesheets include a write-out of their morning routine, their commute, each detail of their class schedule, their commute to an afterschool activity, the activity itself, a commute home, time divided out for studying in each subject, followed by dinner, and their night routine.

Does that sound like a lot? Yes, it probably does, but it can be helpful to those who need that detail.

Have Them Do Work In Their Peak Productivity Time

In high school, this is a little harder because the expectations of a schedule are so rigid, but introducing this concept now will help them in their college or career path.

There is a theory that everyone has a time where they are most productive. For some, it's the crack of dawn. For others, this time might be mid-morning. For others still, this might be afternoon, evening, late at night, etc. Whatever this time is, the brain is doing its best work.

Let them as much as possible if there is any way for your teen to do their homework in these times. If their peak time is the early morning, let them save their most time-intensive subject for that time. If it's late at night, let them go to sleep later, so long as they can at least make sure that they are getting enough sleep.

If your teen goes to college, then they can build their class schedule in such a way that it lets them do their homework in their peak time.

Leave Free Time In Their Day To Day Schedule

What happens to you and your brain if you constantly have to think about a long list of tasks or meetings you need to complete in a day? We all have a few days where things are like this, but if this becomes the case every single day, it can be awful and very stressful. This will also be true for your teen.

School already provides a rigid structure that takes up most of their day. If they have a club, a sport, and several other activities after that, even more of their day is gone to schedule. When it gets so full that they feel like they cannot have a break, then we have stress.

Ask your teen about their schedule. Is it too much? Or do they enjoy it? As adults, they will have the power to put whatever they want into their day, and teaching them as teens that they don't have to pack their schedule with things if they don't want to can help them be more relaxed and well-adjusted as adults.

Prioritize Your Day

When we are teens, schooling will be a top priority. As adults, it's work and sometimes parenting. After this, there are other things that we consider a priority. When your teen adds their priority items to their schedule, make sure that it's in a way where they are made a priority. Start that habit now, so it's easier when they are adults. Some other priorities that might be considered include homework (maybe some subjects take priority over others depending on time, grades, or enjoyment), activities they love, or other obligations.

Get Enough Sleep

Speaking of priorities, let's talk about sleep. Sleep is essential to everyone's ability to function.

As we go through our day-to-day lives, we use the power that our brain has stored. Neurons will degenerate into providing the continuing ability to function. When we sleep, those neurons will regenerate, giving us renewed power for the next day.

When we don't get enough sleep, our neurons won't fully regenerate, and it forces our brain to essentially use a backup generator. Now, we can run on this backup generator for several days before our brain reaches for the neurons that are essential to our function. Still, with each day that the backup generator is running, we are losing our ability to function. The good news is that one good night of sleep erases two or three bad nights, but that feeling of your brain lagging will happen with just one night with poor or too little sleep.

Your child needs to understand the necessity of sleep, and share this knowledge so that they know to prioritize it throughout their lives.

Then, work on a sleep schedule with them. Figure out what their body needs. While eight hours is recommended nationally, many people do fine with as little as six, and others need 10.

Once your teen is sure about what their body needs, make it into a habit that goes into their schedule.

Make Sure That the Schedule Is Enjoyable

If they don't like it, then they won't follow it. Yes, there will be things on there that they don't like, but if the entire schedule is just full of stuff like that, why would they try to follow it?

When the schedule is made, set some parameters (getting enough sleep and time for school) and then let them build it and make sure they will enjoy it. That's the only way the schedule will work.

Try Not To Make Too Many Changes

We want to create a schedule that is easy to follow, not one that's confusing.

Now, as the schedule starts out, there might be some changes as you realize that a commute takes longer (maybe you didn't factor in the time it took to walk to class) or that a specific part of the schedule does better at a different time of day, or something else, but once the kinks are ironed out, make the schedule consistent, with as little change as possible.

Choose the Time Frame You Are Scheduling

Some people do the same thing every day, and others have schedules where they do different things each day of the week. When your teen is making their schedule, have them account for this. Monday and Tuesday might need different schedules.

Try to make each schedule as similar as possible so that they are easy to follow, but make sure that everything is accounted for.

Have A Schedule For the Weekends Too

This one will be a little annoying, but it's essential. A weekend schedule will be looser and probably include lots of free time, but if there are obligations to attend to, even if it's just cleaning your house, make sure they make it onto that schedule.

To-Do List

This tip is stressed in just about every organization and time management topic, which may be annoying, but it's also a testament to just how powerful this is. A to-do list makes it so nothing slips through the cracks, and there are several ways to build one.

First, encourage your teen to keep the syllabus that they get at the beginning of the year. These often contain a course schedule, and information about papers and exams will be on it. If you and your teen want to be on top of things, designate a time to sit down and plan the week. Using a daily or weekly planner can help. Take the time to assign assignments to certain days. Doing this means that the amount of homework is much less overwhelming, and you know when each thing will get done. You can also prepare for tests you know are coming up or big projects that are due in a few weeks.

To help your teen get excited about this and make it visual and easy to follow, use colored pens or highlighters to designate which subject the assignment is for.

If your teen isn't big on planning their week out, a simple to-do list with the assignments they get can help them at least keep track of everything and make sure it gets done.

From here, it helps to take it one step further. At the beginning of each day, sit down and write out a daily to-do list. If your teen has planned their week in advance, then this will be an easy step for them. If your teen adheres to a weekly to-do list, this step will be beneficial to them. This is a time when they can write down assignments, meetings, chores, and anything else they need to get done during the day. Even if your child already keeps a weekly or daily planner, this extra step can help them be prepared for the day as they go into it and stops them from looking at their planner in surprise later.

Pay Attention To How, When, and How Long They Procrastinate

Procrastination is a common pitfall for those who suffer from ADHD. Except, it doesn't happen in the same way it would in a typical brain. First of all, remember that ADHD often relates to functions commonly found in the frontal lobe. One of the things that the frontal lobe is in control of is our attention span. If an activity isn't interesting to us, we don't really want to pay attention, but we might be able to force ourselves to do so. Our teens have even less of a capacity to do that than we do.

Now the flip side is hyperfocus, where your teen is engaged and uninterruptible. They enjoy it, and their brain is almost making too much of the chemical they need. Unless it's interfering with their schedule, this likely isn't what you're worried about.

There is also an issue of dopamine, or the motivation chemical, not being produced as much.

When your teen is procrastinating, have them track it. First of all, how are they procrastinating? Are they taking a long time to prepare for the task? Are they looking at social media? Watching Netflix? Napping (when it isn't needed)?

Next, think about when they are procrastinating? Is it before homework? A particular subject in homework? Is it chores?

Finally, how long do they spend procrastinating? And how big of an effect does it have on their performance? If the effect is minimal to none, then it may be best to leave it alone.

If the effect on their performance is a big one, then something does need to be addressed. These details can also tell you other things.

Procrastination is currently creating more dopamine than doing the work. Is there a way to adjust that?

First, let's look at how your teen might procrastinate? Is it that they take too long to get ready to do the task? Maybe they sit down to study, work for five minutes, and then decide they need a snack. They get up, go get one, and sit back down. After another five minutes, the snack makes them thirsty. They get up, get water, and sit back down. They might decide you need more pencils or paper, coffee, tea, another snack, or something else. Whatever it is, the end result is that they have spent more time getting ready to do the task and less time on the task itself.

To solve this, when you notice that they are having an awful time with this issue, have them write down everything they had to get up and get. The next time, get everything first so that there isn't anything to grab later.

What if their method of procrastination is going on their phone for social media or to watch a movie? Set break times for those apps (most phones will let you lock them for certain lenghs of time). You can also try focus apps or Pomodoro methods to help.

Now, when do they procrastinate? Is it before chores? See if there are certain chores that don't engage them. We will have some tips for those in the next section.

Is it homework? Focus apps can help with this, as can app restrictions and limits. What if it's just a particular subject? If they are procrastinating because they really don't want to touch the material of their least favorite class, have them work on a different one. Sometimes, all we need is to get started. Other times, well, at least the other work is getting done.

Add Something To Mundane Tasks To Make It Interesting

If the tasks are chore related, let them listen to music or a podcast. Let them watch something if it doesn't affect the task. These can increase your child's attention span and ability to get them done.

Now, if that doesn't work, then we need to move to the next step, which is to make everything into a game.

Now, when we talk about the brain having issues with motivation, we are solely speaking about intrinsic motivation. Extrinsic motivation, where the person is motivated by reward, is still able to be used to help you.

The satisfaction of being timed and beating a goal might be enough. If not, try candy, an allowance, privileges that they don't usually get, or a chance to go to an event you know they want to attend. This extrinsic motivation can often bridge the gap.

Try Not To Look Over Their Shoulder

When your teen leaves the nest, they aren't going to have you there to remind them of all of the little things that help them, and they are likely to drop several habits.

Furthermore, if you push ideas onto them, it may make the situation worse. It's not likely that all of these ideas are going to be a perfect fit, and your teen is likely to resist some of them. Move on to the next. Let them figure out their system. This is the best way to make it stick into adulthood.

Goal Setting

Goal setting is the final time management habit that I want to discuss today. First of all, by setting goals, your teen has a reason to think of when her brain tries to resist her.

Second, by talking about goals with another person (you), your teen learns the importance of goal setting and how it can help hold them accountable for meeting those goals.

Finally, goals measure progress. By making progress, we know that we are getting somewhere. When your teen is having a bad day and wants to give up, use her progress toward her goals as motivation.

Time management isn't something your teen struggles with alone. Many people, whether they have ADHD or not, will find challenges in time management. ADHD simply presents some unique challenges to time management. These tips can help navigate some of the challenges.

Another major challenge that ADHD creates for kids is that of organization.

Organization Tips For ADHD

People with ADHD are stereotypically messy. If you think about some of the challenges that they face, it probably isn't surprising to learn that there is some truth to this.

There are issues with focus and motivation, so when it's all combined, things can get… interesting.

How do we navigate these key issues?

After much searching, there turned out to be several tips on how to manage this properly.

Limit How Long You Spend On Decisions

Have you ever noticed that your teen always has a hard time making up their mind? That is a part of executive dysfunction. It's one of the bigger struggles for ADHD. Schedules, to-do lists, and more things where decisions are made ahead of time can really help when it comes to these problems.

When that's not possible, try setting timers. This can be stressful at first, but your teen will likely eventually slide into this.

Try Not To Do Too Much

We already talked about not jamming a schedule so full that there isn't room to just sit down and breathe. Now, we are going to talk about overcommitment. When getting your teen to organize, they might overcommit to a task and either spend way more hours on it than they should, or they might run out of motivation halfway through.

When you start teaching them this concept, guide them. When they talk about big projects, see if you can talk them into scaling back or planning to do this in stages. Show enthusiasm, but also remind them that this might not be the perfect fix they are hoping for.

Work Together

This doesn't mean that you and your teen are working together on their homework.

Have you ever gone to a coffee shop or library to get some work done? I certainly have, and I've been tempted to look on my phone while I'm there. But unlike when I'm at home, and no one is watching, I don't do that. There is something about having others who are there and working with you that just makes everything so much more engaged. Use an effect like this to your advantage. Sit with your teen and work. You could be doing work, creating a budget, looking at new recipes, or whatever you need to get done that will help your teen. If you are working, they are more likely to naturally do so too!

Keep Everything Bright And Visual

I cannot stress this enough. Have things that are visual. Bright, visible things are much easier for the brain to take in. When your child has ADHD, it makes a difference. Label things. Have them label things.

Color code stuff. Do whatever you need to do to help your child make it visual in a way that they can work with.

Help Your Teen Fight Clutter

There are so many things out there that we can buy that we will never use again. These just take up space and become a mess that we have to deal with.

Your teen might have spending money of their own. They might find that when they see it in a store, it's cute. So, they take it home, they put it on their desk or on a shelf, and it's never handled again. Despite this, they will fight to keep it until the day they die.

This is a step that your teen will need either your assistance or the assistance of others.

First of all, when they are buying things, don't let them shop alone if you can help it. If you aren't there, let their friends be their moral compass. When they consider buying something, ask them what use it is going to have. If they don't seem to have an answer, try to convince them to put it back.

Now, when they are trying to clean and declutter their room, either be there or have someone else that they are close with to be there. Be the logic to their emotion if they try to justify the item's place.

Manage The Amount Of Projects Your Teen Is Trying To Do

Hyperfocus and a sudden stop in motivation can lead to massive projects that are halfway finished. Obviously, this is a struggle. They take up time and space, but it doesn't feel like there is anything you can do.

Try to guide them to two to three projects at a time. Have them manage them. It can help them get control and finish things without also feeling overwhelmed by the projects they already have.

Use A Timer To Organize

A big mess isn't going to be easy to clean, and spending time on it can feel exhausting. When you have ADHD, and all you see is a big mess, it can be overwhelming to think about cleaning it. Your teen might procrastinate as a result of this.

A popular way that people have fought this is by setting a ten to fifteen-minute timer every day and using that timer as the time they have to clean and declutter. If their room or other spaces are really messy, 15 minutes may admittedly not seem like enough, but if it's done every day, they will catch up to the mess, and it helps to prevent future messes from getting out of control.

Have a Centralized Spot For Things You Need To Leave The House

This has the power to benefit everyone in your home, and it's a great thing for your teen later. Have some command hooks, a basket, or another method for everyone to store their keys, wallet, mask, and anything else they might need to leave the house.

Find Some Different Organization Methods Online With Your Teen

This last tip is for if you and your teen are really struggling to come up with a system of organization. If, no matter what you do, you can't seem to figure out one that works for your house, then it's time to look online. Do this with your teen and try to help get them excited for a step like this. It can help them get organized now and understand how to look for resources when they need them in the future.

Organization and time management are not innate skills in any of us, but they can be learned. It can be hard to pick up when ADHD is involved, but implementing some extra strategies can really help!

Chapter Five
Money Management

At the beginning of her adult life, Lisa took out several credit cards and a few loans. She spent it with little thought and no budget.

By the time she was 25, it had caught up to her. She nearly had to move back in with her parents because she didn't have enough money for rent or other expenses. At this point, she was able to save herself and pull herself back up on her feet. She got married and had her son, and she'd been able to give her son a life with all his necessities met and several other luxuries, like vacations, sports, new clothes, and a car. Her son James hasn't had to worry about money, and she worries that he will make the same mistakes.

Her husband has told her not to worry. It's just a part of James' ADHD, and he will grow out of it. Lisa still worries.

She needs to teach James the basics of money management, and soon. Otherwise, he might head down the same path, and with his ADHD, he might not realize it until it's too late.

Understandably, you probably want your teen to avoid the same fate. You don't want them going down a path where they overspend, go into debt, and get themselves into a mess that they can't get out of.

A lot of it will come from putting the responsibility in their hands early, which we are going to start talking about.

Get Them The Proper Supplies

What does your teen need to manage money?

First, they are going to need a way to keep a budget, which can be a physical checkbook, a notebook, an excel spreadsheet, or really whatever is easiest for your teen. In addition to this, they are going to want a calculator and possibly some writing utensils. If your teen primarily earns cash, then they either will need a bank account for cash storage or a system to budget the cash at home. Some money experts recommend using cash envelopes for budgeting. The pro is that you have a visual representation of how much money you have. On the other hand, it does create some risk.

Let Them Get A Job

In order to learn how to handle money, they have to be able to earn it. A part-time job can be worked around school and can be an excellent outlet for physical exercise. Plus, they can get something to put on their resume.

Having a job is something we all have to do for most of our lives. There are benefits to learning how to handle a job as a teenager, especially as someone who has ADHD. There are many customer service jobs that involve a lot of tasks and a lot of business, and someone with ADHD, whose brain is constantly moving to the next thing, can find a good groove here.

A job will let them earn money that you can use to teach them. Many of the tips here are dependent on them having some sort of stream of income, whether it's a physical job, online work, or under-the-table work.

Guide Your Teen In Creating Their First Budget

Creating your first budget can be overwhelming, regardless of how your brain might be composed. It's always a good idea to be there that first time so that you can explain some of the things that need to be done.

First of all, how do you decide when to budget? People who are salaried or know in advance how much money they are going to make have the advantage of planning in advance. Your teen might not have that, especially if they have a changing schedule. If this is the case, get them into the habit of budgeting no more than 48 hours later. When you get your kid to budget, start with their needs. Do they have any bills that need to be paid? What about clothes? School supplies? School lunches? As they get older, they might want certain clothes or supplies, and they might want to get lunch off-campus. These would be great uses for their budget.

Next, consider the wants they might have. Some things, like certain clothes, are technically a need and a want and can be budgeted for before this category. Their wants might be things like a new gaming system, a new phone, or something else that they are looking to get.

There is also the matter of saving for bigger purchases like a car or college if that's the route they want to go. If you aren't sure what money is going to be brought in, always set aside the proper amounts for bills and then go into the other items and assign them a certain percentage of the budget.

After you have sat down and discussed this, set aside some time to go over it with them in the future and hold them accountable to stick to it, most banking is online now, so it's much easier to be aware of what's going in and out.

Talk To Them About Long-Term Goals

Like we talked about above in the budgeting sections, there are going to be long-term saving goals for your child that are going to help them in the long run.

Most children want a car as they hit their legal driving age. While some families can afford to help out with this, some can't. If your teen is starting to make money, then start talking to them about this as one of their long-term goals.

Another potential long-term goal is college. Today, we do live in a place where a college degree isn't always needed, but for many, it is the route they want to take. If your teen is interested in college, this is another thing to be saving for.

Saving doesn't automatically sound appealing, and we have to remember that a part of ADHD is impulsive decisions, which can be made with money.

First, the goals should be reasonable and set by your teen more than they are set by you.

Next, make sure that your teen has a visible way to track their budget. The money envelope system is helpful for this because money for spending is separate from saving. There are just two issues. One issue is a security concern of having all cash assets. The other is that a lot of shopping is done online.

If your teen isn't interested in making online purchases, and you know that the safety of their money is practically guaranteed, then this might be a viable option.

Another great way to make their spending visual is to install their bank app on their phone. It can track money and often holds spending charts. If you think it will help, you can all draw these charts onto a dry-erase board.

The final thing you can do is start a savings account for your teen. This separates the money that they are supposed to save so that it can't be easily spent.

Another component of this is to make the goals visual.

If your teen is looking forward to a car, start researching cars that they might want. Do some research online with your teen so that they learn some sales terminology, get an idea of what features they might want, and they know what to look for in cars. Used cars are often the way to go in terms of a first car, but to get one also requires extra knowledge (including how to tell if you are being scammed). All of this research can help make your teen excited to reach their goal. As they save, help them envision their dream car. It makes the goal real and appealing.

Another common long-term saving goal is college. A lot of the steps are going to be the same, and they are important for more reasons than just budgeting. First, what major is your child interested in heading toward? Most colleges don't carry every single major that there is.

Next, do they want to be in the state or out of state? Do they understand the cost difference between the two? Finally, what schools specifically are they looking at? Many schools will list information about their cost of attendance online, and your teen can easily view this information. While college itself is scary, campus and dorm room pictures, researching the town they might go to, and gaining knowledge on their program can get them excited and help motivate them to save.

The same formula works best with most long-term goals. Researching the goal can help your teen get excited about it, and it can also help them get motivated to save up so that it can happen. Long-term goals will be, in some way, a part of our budget forever, so we need to start thinking about them at a younger age.

Explaining Debt

Does your teen understand what it means to be in debt? Do they know what kind of consequences are associated with it?

Loans are a tool, and this tool has to be used wisely. If we aren't wise about our loan decisions, then we end up in deep trouble. The impulsive nature of ADHD might create a situation where your child readily uses their card and doesn't think about the consequence of doing so. We don't want them to leave our house without the knowledge of how to properly make decisions about loans and debt.

First, let's talk about loans. Loans are sometimes just a part of life. People get loans for a car, college, and houses all of the time. The tricky part about loans isn't the loans themselves but the interest. In the long run, you pay more money over time.

A trick that I have found helpful when teaching about money and loans is to ask, "will this help you advance in your life?"

A car loan probably will if it helps you get a good car that outlives the loan. What about student loans? They are a pain, but they will absolutely help you advance. Home loans? Yup, those too!

Now, what about a loan for the latest phone? Probably not, unless your teen is making money through their device (after all, many phones have the capacity of a professional camera). Purchases that are for fun should probably not be made into a loan.

Again, this is a part of fighting the natural impulsive tendencies of ADHD.

Next, let's talk about credit cards. Again, they are a great tool, but they have to be used wisely.

Teach your teen that they should expect to pay the balance in full each month, as that is what keeps them out of debt and helps build their credit score. Also, some credit cards are better than others, and it's helpful to understand that too.

When this knowledge fails to help them, then they experience natural consequences, which we will talk about at the end of this chapter.

Subscriptions

Subscriptions have a unique teaching power that you can't really find anywhere else at that young age.

Bills are a part of adult life, but when we are teenagers, there aren't many bills to consider. How do we then teach the concept of bills?

One way to do this is through subscription services. These come in many forms. There are things like Netflix and other streaming services. There are also things like subscription boxes. If your family already pays for streaming services, then subscription boxes may be the way to go.

The joy of a subscription box is that it can be catered to things that your child is interested in. This could be books, art, cooking, or other hobbies. This gives them something visual to look forward to every month while creating a bill for them to manage. You can get a couple of boxes to provide them with the experience of having a couple of bills, but keep in mind that this might create a problem of too much clutter.

If your teen struggles to budget for this appropriately, then we move into the phase of natural consequences.

Natural Consequences

Now that I have brought them up a few times, it's time to talk about what natural consequences mean. Money is great when it comes to this.

There are many times in our children's lives when we don't need to rely on methods of discipline or punishment. Their actions have natural consequences or something that logically follows their action. For children with ADHD, this is actually an excellent way for them to learn, as a lot of punishment and discipline do not have the intended effect. Instead, a child with ADHD is likely to focus on what happened or the negative of the punishment or discipline method, and the actual lesson will be lost. On the other hand, a natural consequence creates a cause-and-effect relationship that won't be forgotten so easily.

How does this work with loans? Your child now has to pay these back, and they lose more money each month to bills. If they don't pay them back, then it hurts their credit score, and it could get them in legal trouble. Plus, if they buy something like a new phone, and don't pay the loan back, then they often get another loan for the next new phone.

What about credit card statements? Same thing. If your child uses their card too much, they will eventually hit their limit, and if it's not paid on time, the card will get declined. It won't come back until your teen has paid what they need to pay.

What about subscriptions and streaming services? What happens if your child doesn't save the way that they are supposed to, and they end up not having enough to cover the subscription? Most subscriptions can be paused for a month.

These are all natural consequences of their actions. If they use money improperly, then they have to face the fact that they now need to make sacrifices and cuts. They lose out on things that they enjoy.

I understand that it might be really tempting to step in and save them, but you aren't doing them any favors. They can dig themselves out of this hole, and it's best that they are learning now and not later.

A lot of success is found when support and guidance are offered, but not assistance.

Money is something that many people feel is too tight today and a lot of people have to create budgets. Your teen is going to be no exception.

Understanding the basics now can prepare them for the future, which is often less kind.

It's going to feel interesting when your teen talks about getting loans or wanting a car, but these things are normal and great learning opportunities.

Chapter Six
At Home Maintenance

As adults, we can technically call a repairman for anything we want. We can also hire a cleaning agency or housekeeper. We can hire someone to organize our money and our documents. There is a service for pretty much every adult need you could have. The trouble? That's expensive. Not only is it cheaper, but it is much faster to do it yourself.

Now, what about your teen? They have ADHD. These things are going to be tough, right? They have such a hard time taking care of things at home; how are they going to fare when they get their own place?

While I think this is a valid concern, I don't want you to worry.

To illustrate my point, I want you to meet Emma. Today, Emma is a stay-at-home mom. She cooks, cleans, balances the budget, sorts documents, and with the help of her husband, she keeps a household for four children (two of which have ADHD) afloat.

If you met her in college, you would be surprised. Emma left home with no ideas about things like how to do laundry or make a pot of noodles. Her parents always thought of her as scatterbrained, and though her mom made a few small attempts to teach Emma some of these skills, she always gave up in the end. This didn't benefit Emma, who struggled a lot at first and had to ask her roommates for a lot of help.

At the age of 22, a year away from graduation, Emma was finally diagnosed with ADHD. She now understood why her parents had such a hard time teaching her what she needed to know for her adult life. She was able to use sources that she found to teach herself how to do these tasks in a memorable way.

Now that her kids are starting to enter their teens, she wants them all to have the knowledge of how to successfully take care of their home, especially her kiddos with ADHD. How does she make sure of that?

"Life Hacks" That Can Help Those Who Have ADHD

House management from one of Emma's children to the next might look different. Her typical brain children might do things differently from their siblings (who may also differ in house maintenance) and from each other. They may even find some of these tips helpful too! For those who have ADHD, these tips can make things really easy!

Cooking Tip: Use An Instant Pot For Making Meals

If your child has ADHD, this could be a great moving away present for when they move out. Instapots have the capacity to do a lot!

If your child struggles with cooking, it can help. A lot of Instapot recipes work by simply throwing a bunch of ingredients in the pot and setting it. While your child goes about their day, or they are at home relaxing, they can have their next meal cooking.

Set Up Your Kitchen Space So That Like Things Are Grouped Together

If you have ever worked a food service job, you might understand the importance of this right off the bat. Think about it. If you worked at a pizza place, it wouldn't make any sense to have dough on one side of the store, sauce on another, and then all of the toppings at another end of the store. It's all lined up for ease of use.

If you and your child are able to set up their home in a similar way, then it will make it easier. This might mean having the knives and cutting boards grouped together. It might mean that the spices are right next to the stove and oven. The baking dishes are stored under the oven, where a person can easily grab them. Water bottles are right next to the fridge, where you can grab one to fill it up. If you enjoy coffee or tea in the mornings, everything you need to make it is within your reach!

This makes it very easy to accomplish things in the morning. You don't have to spend time looking for something, and therefore, you have fewer opportunities to get distracted in the morning.

Easy Make Appliances

An Instapot is just one example.

The world comes up with a lot of crazy gadgets that we don't ever think we would need. There are apple slicers, strawberry pitters, Keurigs, electric kettles, panini makers, and more.

If it helps your teen, encourage them to get it for themselves. Whatever will help make things easier for them is worth the investment!

Organizational systems

Keep in mind that when your teen is off living on their own, they aren't going to have you there. This means that if they get distracted in the morning, you aren't going to pull them back and remind them that they need to be focusing on getting ready.

Part of this will be eliminating opportunities to get distracted from the task at hand. One of the things that can play a role in distraction is too many things that don't have a home. Clutter and mess can take up a lot of space and confuse the mind. Try to help them find places for their belongings as much as possible. When it's not possible, invest in a few spaces that are designated for clutter so that it's out of sight.

Color Code Everything!

The ADHD brain processes visual information the best. It's time to take full advantage of this. Color coding can go for your laundry baskets (different colors depending on whether it's lights, colors, or darks), drawers, and desk space; you name it.

If you are trying to color-code drawers in some way, use electrical tape. It sticks really well, but if you happen to be renting your space (or you just don't want to damage your property), they don't leave any damage behind. You can also buy it in fun colors.

Marie Kondo Methods

Let's talk about two ideas that Marie Kondo had that someone with ADHD can bring into their life.

The first is the method that she chooses for decluttering. Is the item serving a purpose? Have you used it in the last two weeks? Does it spark joy? If you can't answer anything here with a yes, then it needs to go. These three simple questions can help you decide whether or not to keep an item in your house. This streamlines the process, and it can help you get rid of so many things.

The next popular method she has is of folding things. When you follow this, items are folded in such a way that they can stand up when they are bunched together. This means that when you open a drawer, it's all visible. You can see everything you need for the occasion.

Once again, this can help someone with ADHD adhere to keeping things visual. It also helps them take more advantage of their wardrobe.

Make Use Of Visual Reminder Methods

One huge example of visual reminders is post-it notes. You can stick these anywhere, and they can remind you of things that are going on. Another example is using window markers, which are good for your mirror as well. You can write with them and then take them off like a window cleaner.

Maintaining a day-to-day life with the challenge of ADHD is manageable. You just need to know a few extra tips. Our next topic is similar.

Life Paperwork

No one tells us just how much paperwork is involved when you become an adult. We need to keep track of identity documents, financial documents, and so much more. How does your teen handle this?

First, there must be an organizational system. A filing cabinet is the best, most visual option for this. Use picture labels instead of writing it out if you can! Some things can now be kept digitally, which we are going to talk about below.

Identity Documents

This is your birth certificate, passport, social security card, and to some extent, your driver's license. Your teen's driver's license should be with them at all times. Everything else should be stored in a place that is as safe as possible. Try to lock it away if you can.

Some things on these lists can be stored online, but not these. There are watermarks and a host of security things stored within these documents that people will look for. You won't be able to find these things online.

Medical Documents

Medical documents are tricky. There are some that you shouldn't worry about, and some you should keep for a long time.

Many of your insurance documents can be scanned and uploaded online or to a server. The same is true for any yearly exam, be it physical, dental, or vision. Keep a physical copy of the most recent and have your teen add it to their filing system.

Medical bills (from hospitals) should be scanned ASAP. Your teen is going to want to retain physical copies at least until the debt is paid. Even after that, retain scanned copies, and your teen will want to be able to access them. Hospital investigations happen often, and your teen will want their documents in hand.

Your teen will also want to have physical documentation of their ADHD. Many employers are willing to accommodate, provided that there is proof that the person has the disorder. Doctor's notes, a record of diagnosis, or another legal/medical document that talks about their ADHD should suffice.

Housing Documents

This refers to anything related to your current housing situation. Today, most young adults rent their homes first. When you rent a home, you are going to want a copy of a renters agreement, bank statements, checklist, and information about devices in the house (like smoke detectors, carbon monoxide detectors, the dishwasher, etc.). Further, it is best to retain any safety procedures that the landlord would like followed, any legal issues that need to be tended to, and the checklist of damages that existed when they moved in.

Today, these documents may already exist online, in which case you have a pdf that you can easily keep track of. If the original copy is paper, though, you should save that for the duration that you live there.

Now, if they own a home, they are going to want all of your information for that as well. In this case, it doesn't need to be on hand. Owning a home is a more stable situation. If you damage something, you fix it without jumping through hoops. You will have a deed, but you won't need to sign legal forms with a landlord. And, you won't need to keep track of a housing contract, which many people have to do.

For these papers, having electronic copies is fine.

Car Documents

There are probably some good odds that your teen either has a car or has plans to get one in the future (even if it's the distant future). There will be a lot of documents for their vehicle, but what do you keep?

You will want to keep what the dealer gives you. Keep it in hard copy for about a year before you scan it and try to go digital with it.

You should also keep a copy of registration information, lease information if a loan was used, the title, and your insurance information.

Keep insurance information and registration information in the car. The rest can be filed until it can be digitized.

Purchase Receipts

There used to be a time when you would want to carry all of your receipts and keep a hold of them for your taxes. Electronic banking has mostly stopped this habit. In addition to always having access to the charges on your accounts, if you need a receipt, you can get one emailed to you.

For those who have ADHD, a pile of receipts can look like an overwhelming mess of clutter. It's hard to sort through, and they may not even need it. Receipts can be scanned and digitized if they would like, but they don't have to be.

The only time your teen should need to keep a receipt is if they made the purchase for his workplace. Any receipt copies don't have to be kept for more than three years.

Rental and Homeowner Repair and Renovation

If they live in a rental and something breaks or a renovation takes place, then the landlord usually pays for that, except in particular circumstances. For these, if they sign any agreements with the contracted company or the landlord, then they should keep either physical or scanned copies, just in case they are needed. They should only need to keep these for a year, though.

If they own a home, then this is going to look a little different. They are going to want to keep these records longer as they might matter when it comes to a tax return. The recommendation is to keep copies (physical or online) for about five years.

Pay Stubs

Most pay stubs are electronically delivered now. If your teen still gets paper stubs, they only need to keep them for about a year or until tax season comes.

Power, Water, and Other Utilities

The bills for these may be either online or in paper form. If they are online and you receive PDFs, then store those safely. They may also be found online through an account they have with the utility company, in which case they don't need to worry about it.

Most utility companies still send bills through the mail, though, so they may have paper copies to deal with. It's best to keep them for about a year. They might not need them for tax purposes, but your now-adult may need to check them for errors by comparing them, or you might notice that something extra is running in the house when it doesn't need to be, and it's driving your bills up.

Credit Card Information

You don't really have to keep these for too long. When your teen gets a credit card, teach them to check the statement to make sure that all of the charges are correct, and then they can be thrown away.

Property and Investment Information

Investments are an exciting topic and probably one you're going to want to discuss with your teen. The recommendation is to always start as soon as possible with at least a retirement investment.

Then, you might go bigger and continue to invest from there. Explain the purpose of investments so your teen understands. For these, they need to have a good hold of the investment information for about three years, just in case the IRS takes a look and asks for the info.

Properties aren't likely to be something your teen has right away unless they inherit something from the family, but they do fall into the same category as investments.

Tax records

If your teen is underage but has a job, they are going to have tax returns to deal with. You might be able to keep them online, so you don't have to deal with a paper copy, but you should keep hold of them for at least three years.

Loan Records

If your teen isn't 18 yet, they probably won't have these, but when they do, they should keep their payment records for up to three years and the record of a paid-off loan for seven years.

What To Do With All Of This Information?

Your teen probably doesn't have to deal with most of these things just yet, but they will soon! Given that information on these papers isn't common knowledge, it's all presented here.

When people get a hold of important papers, one of two things are bound to happen. They either keep it for twenty years or throw it away immediately. Having a system in place when your teen moves out can help avoid either of these.

Start devising one for your own papers and let your teen help. Seeing this model early can help them know what to do in the future.

When it comes time for your teen to move out, help them first set up a filing cabinet. With each file, have the information on what it contains, how long the items inside need to be kept, and the last date they went through it. If you, and later your teen, are able to set aside monthly time to go through these documents, a couple of folders at a time, then you can generally keep up on the paperwork that comes with life.

Clean Homes

It's often been said that people with ADHD are naturally messier. Maybe that's true; however, it doesn't mean that those with ADHD can't keep a clean home. If your teen is prone to mess, then let's look at some things that might help them.

Sort Through Mail and Papers Every Day

Mail and paperwork can pile up fast, and with ADHD, trying to sort through all of it at the end of the week just sounds awful and like a disaster waiting to happen. Now, if you do it each day, it won't pile up. You can model this behavior to your teen and let them know why you do it!

Have A Weekly Chore Plan

No one likes having to spend all day cleaning their house, and if you have ADHD, it might not get done at all. Instead of trying to do it all in one day, set up a weekly plan for what gets done and when.

You can do this in a planner or an app, but take time to sit with your teen, write down all of the chores that need to be done in the house, and write down when the day they are going to be done. When they still live at home, also write down who is going to do them. When your teen is on their own, they will already have this practice down!

Keep Laundry In the Laundry Room

In addition to being helped by color-coded baskets, your teen is likely to find some use in having it all in the laundry room. With the baskets right next to the washer, your teen can simply toss in the basket when it gets full and start it when they need to.

Kitchen Maintenance

First, try to have your teen make a habit of rinsing their dish every meal. By doing this, they are stopping the sink from becoming a problem. Next, have them make sure the dishwasher runs every night, and make it a point to have it be put away in the morning so that dirty dishes can go right in. Try not to purchase too many things that need to be hand-washed, as it just happens to make things more complicated.

Next, when teaching about a clean fridge, have them first understand the importance of fridge maintenance and teach them the smell test. Cleaning the fridge out at least once a month with disinfectant is essential, and your teen might be more engaged by listening to music or watching the difference between a dirty and clean fridge.

Bathrooms

A tip your teen might find helpful is to turn the water on for the shower and run it as hot as possible for about ten minutes. The steam this creates will loosen a lot of stain buildup.

Now with that done, most of the mess can be wiped away easily!

Understandably, having your teen living on their own might be a stressful time for you. It may help when they are set up and know how to take care of their home in the future. Right now, a lot of things probably seem like they are far off from happening, but the sooner we start modeling behaviors, the better they will be for the future.

Chapter Seven
I Can't Remember

ADHD often comes with memory deficits. When you learn that memory is also centered in the frontal lobe, that information probably won't surprise you.

Being able to remember important details is often essential to making sure that we are getting our work done in a timely fashion and that we are on top of things. Right now, you are likely primarily noticing your child's memory deficit in school. As they get into the workforce, it's likely to impact them there too. There are several methods in the school and working world that can help your teen get a head start and make up the slack that the frontal is creating. Starting to teach them now while they are in school can ensure that they become great habits in the future.

Some General Memory Tricks

Let's start with the basics.

Make An Emotional Connection

When your child is learning about something, one thing that can help them retain it is to make an emotional connection with the information. While this might be tough in math class, in classes like English and history, it's easy. English papers are written with emotion, and a personal story often gets the teacher's attention and stands out in a good way among the sea of papers they have to grade. Your child can also connect better to the material that they were working on.

In history class, your child might connect by learning about relatives or the emotional stories of people and what they experienced during significant historical events.

Make It Unique

When your child is struggling to pick up school material, help them by getting creative with how you might help them study it.

You can use Pinterest or google for some inspiration and go from there! Flashcards, rereading the text, and other traditional methods haven't been helping, so what will? The more creative the idea, the better it can be absorbed!

Get Your Senses Involved

When your teen is in school and receiving the information, they are already engaging two basic senses: sight and hearing. See if you can engage the other three. In science, perhaps they are learning about different smell reactions. If it's safe, see if you can create the small. In history, they might be learning about a new historical event. See if you can't find an area where they might be able to imagine themselves in that event.

Sensory experiences can go a long way in making our memory do its job and remember things. You are making up to five different connections with the material.

Make Use Of Movement

Motion can engage the memory as well.

Let's say, for example, that your child is looking to learn a complicated math formula. Put it on a dry erase board. Have them draw arrows, trace steps, and move their way through the process.

Use Mnemonics and Word Tricks

Schools often use this a lot already. You might have heard of PEMDAS or, Please Excuse My Dear Aunt Sally for the way to remember the proper order for basic math equations. These tend to stick in our minds because it's a pattern. For an odd reason, we tend to attach to those.

Create as many as you want and make them as wacky as you want. They tend to stick even better when you do.

Engage Your Focusing Skills

The frontal lobe also controls our ability to focus, and that can sometimes be the cause of our issues. Focus isn't just going to magically appear because we want it to, especially when ADHD is involved. Occasionally, we need to get creative about how we do this. One thing you can do is try to meditate. Spend some time focusing on nothing. When the time is up, your brain is refreshed, and you can try again!

Another thing you can try to do is engage a different part of your brain. An easy way to do this is to toss a ball between your hands and catch it. This repeated action makes it so that you can restructure your thoughts a bit.

Music can help. Try music with little to no words or a simple tune. Focus music that lasts for several hours can help with longer studying sessions.

If the problem is a lack of focus, then that part needs to be taken care of before anything else!

Take a Break and Get Some Fresh Air

If you have spent an hour trying to get the information together, then a 110 to 20-minute walk is likely in your best interest. The fresh air has a healing effect on our body, and it can remove the stress blocks from our mind that may be causing our memory to fall short. Furthermore, by taking the time to walk away, we are letting the jumbled information fall away from our brains.

It gives us a clean slate, and we can start over on our work. When we do this, the stress blocks are gone, and our brain gets to recreate the map of its thoughts. It may now create it in such a way that we can easily recall what we were initially struggling with.

Exercises For The Memory

There are many things that we can do in our environment and for ourselves that will help out memory.

Create A Dedicated Space For Your Teen To Work

We've talked about how this relates to other chapters, but let's explore its specific connection to memory.

Our brains respond differently depending on their environment. In a previous example, we talked about what happens when we go to a coffee shop. We might want to stop working, but there is a certain amount of peer pressure around us that won't let that happen. There is another factor in play as well.

Do you regularly go to a coffee shop to work? If you do, your brain has likely made this a "designated workspace." This means that your focus and work will improve, including the speed at which you do it and how well you might remember it.

If you are able to create a space like this in your teen's home, it can improve their memory.

In order to make this work, this space needs to only be dedicated to working. It's not going to be a space to also eat, for entertainment, or a space to sit and get ready for the day. Doing those things in this space can confuse the brain and lessen the effect that the area will have on the work.

Once this space is designated, try to make it as distraction-free as possible. Have all of the materials nearby. With an environment that is there to support their needs, your teen is likely to run into fewer problems overall.

Create Signals For The Brain

Allow me to introduce you to Ivan Pavlov. Pavlov is credited with the discovery of classical conditioning. In his experiment, he discovered that when a dog is presented with food (which causes them to start drooling) and another stimulus (a bell in this case), the dog will eventually associate the bell with food and will drool at the sound of the bell, even with no food present.

We are able to classically condition ourselves if we would like to. When it's time for your teen to study or do homework, with their permission, create something that leads to classical conditioning. In this case, you might try a particular white noise sound, like a fan or the ocean. You can also try focus music.

Whatever the sound is, start playing it a couple of minutes before they begin their homework or studying session. Then, continue to let it play as they work.

As a bonus, if your teen finds that they are struggling with focusing in school, they can play this sound to help them focus. You can have the doctor include this in their IEP or 504 plan.

Measure Out Progress and New Work

Having a way to quantify progress can help keep your teen from becoming discouraged.

A good, simple, visual way to do this is to keep a dry erase board in their study area. Using this dry-erase board on normal homework days might mean that you write down each subject and the work you are going to do for it. As you do the work, you cross it off until there is nothing left.

On days where one subject is particularly demanding or difficult, let that subject take over the board. Write down every little thing that has to be dealt with and cross it off one by one.

When they enter the workforce, this technique can be really helpful to them as well. Each time they complete a task they need to do or a part of a project, they can cross it off!

The visual is a reminder to the brain that, first of all, a lot has been done and that there is a lot to go!

Help Them Create A Mental Map Of The Work

Okay, so here is one of the good things about school. When you are introduced to a new topic, it often isn't completely new. It's likely linked to another topic that you studied in class. One way to help your teen remember all of this information is to link it together.

In math, this is easier because mathematical knowledge tends to build. Have your child start the new topic by reviewing previous, relevant material and drawing any needed connections. This starts up some background knowledge that will help them remember their new lessons, and it gives them material to draw from and connect to when they are struggling.

In English, your child is learning new things all about the same language. One thing you can do is have your child give examples of new concepts but always use the same reading. It can be an excerpt from their favorite book, which can be engaging, but use it to have them point out as many examples as possible about what they are learning. When there aren't any examples available, have them rewrite sentences about what they are learning.

In history, create a timeline. When did this news even happen? During what time period? Compared to other events, when did this fall?

Aim For Understanding Before They Memorize It

Your child may be able to memorize the entire math formula, and yet they might not understand anything about it. Before we have them memorize this information, they need to be able to comprehend it. What are some things we can do about this?

Have them work through parts of the sequence at a time. Have them draw things out or use objects to demonstrate. Have them try to relate it to themselves or other things in their life. There are quite a few options available, and the best one will depend on how your teen processes things.

Once you are sure that they fully understand the material, then you can dive into memorization strategies.

Practice

The saying "practice makes perfect" is absolutely true when it comes to remembering information.

Have your child practice as much as possible, and try to make it fun. Invest in a big dry erase board for math practice. Have them retry (safe) science experiments at home, or at least watch videos about the cool aspects of what they are learning.

In subjects like English and history, create a Kahoot and get their friends to play before a test. Kahoot is an online quiz game used by teachers. It ranks people by their correct answers and how fast they get them.

Anything that creates opportunities to practice what they are learning is going to improve their memory.

Create Info Sheets

These can be math formulas, scientific facts, the periodic table, a list of vocabulary, a history timeline, what different English sentence parts are, and whatever else your teen may need to stay on top of their studies. It might seem counterintuitive for their memory, but having it close by to stare at can help. It also stresses comprehension over basic meaning.

Understandably, you might wonder if this is going to be helpful in the long run, but most college tests are online and open-note, thanks to technology. Students are often allowed their notes too. Once they get a job, having notes on hand will likely be a part of it.

Now, in high school, things are a little more strict, but it's always worth it to talk to your teacher. In some cases, you might be able to get it into their IEP or 504.

Don't Forget The Highlighters.

Information is often better presented visually or verbally. It's rare for someone with ADHD to do their best work while staring at a block of text. Find colorful highlighters. Use a brand that has several different colors to offer.

Now, you can't usually write all over a school book. What you can do is attach translucent paper and highlight all over that. You might also be able to rent the book online and use that to make your highlights.

Your child can use whatever system of highlighting works best for them. They might choose to only highlight the important information. They might highlight every other paragraph or alternate colors on paragraphs so they have an easier time reading them. They may also highlight the topics within the chapter.

Highlighting doesn't have to be reserved for textbooks. Let your child feel free to highlight their notes, handouts, and homework as needed.

The simple act can help to make the information visual to your child.

Schedule Reviews

This can help make tasks like preparing for tests feel less daunting. Schedule different review times for each subject, and use these to revisit parts of the information your child has been learning.

You might use these times to go over the information that was harder for them to understand. You might use this time to go over things that maybe didn't make sense initially but do with the extra time. You might use this time to go over things they learned at the beginning of the unit that you know will still be on the test.

These review times can be serious, or a game can be made out of them. They can be conducted in the usual space your child has, or you can decide to go outside or to a park or a coffee shop. You can lead these, or your child can. Whatever route you take will depend on how your child's brain naturally processes information.

Study Your Teen's Style

You don't want to embark on this journey and discount the things that work well for your teen already. If they have certain things that they do that help them learn, work these into some of these tips. This is what your child's brain is already naturally doing. The goal is to enhance it.

These exercises start in school, and then they can continue into the adult world with your teen.

While your teen may not need the knowledge of every subject from school as they enter the adult world, there are skills like time and project management, information absorption, and memory techniques that they will take with them to the adult world. Their adult life and workplace may require it. What other skills about being a student can we teach that will help them in their adult life?

ADHD Study Tips

When your child brings home a bad grade, you might think that they just need more time than the average student to study. While this is a sensible explanation, it isn't an accurate one. An ADHD brain doesn't work like a traditional one, so traditional methods might not be of much help.

This is true now, and it will be true for their jobs later. What are some things that they can do?

Engage In Active Studying

This is something that experts in education recommend for college students, and it's especially helpful to people with ADHD. We discussed the weakness of the textbook for those with ADHD in a previous section. However, that is often the most popular method of studying.

Think instead of making tests, using flashcards, or doing group study. These methods feel overwhelming at first, but they lead to better retention in the long run. These are called active study methods, and it essentially forces your brain to engage with the information you have just given it.

Record Lectures

If you are worried that teachers won't allow recording, then try to get it into your teen's IEP or 504. Recording lectures means that, first of all, if your child feels that they missed important information, they have something to go back to. Second of all, if your child wants, they can listen to the lecture again, identify the important information, and get it either rewritten or highlighted in their notes. This is active learning as they are actively attending to and identifying the information.

Make Technology a Part Of the Routine

Technology has so much to offer the ADHD world. Many apps have been created to make our lives easier, and we should take advantage of them. There are note-taking apps like Notability, flashcard apps (like Chegg), and apps for quizzes (like Quizlet). Using technology for this can help to streamline the process and get your child working faster. Part of studying will be efficiency.

Don't Let Your Child Cram.

Cramming is never a good strategy, especially when you have ADHD. First of all, if your teen plans to cram and save it all to the last minute, they have no backup for a bad day with their focus. Second, trying to study for long periods of time hurts everyone's focus. Third, spreading it out gives your teens a chance to better process things. Alternatively, have them stay on top of studying throughout the year. This way, there is little panic and routine disruption when a test is coming up.

Environment Tip: Essential Oil Diffuser

Using an essential oil diffuser can help your child focus if it's the right scent. Studies show that mint, citrus, and eucalyptus all have powerful focus effects. You can get a diffuser and let the smell come into the room for your teen to use. These smells may eventually also lead to a classical conditioning effect, and your child can easily take them to school and rub them on their wrist as needed.

These scents can also help with stress levels, especially when they are around comforting places for your teen.

Light Sugars

Our brain uses up a surprising amount of energy each day. Because your teen has ADHD, they might even be using double the amount of energy that their peers are for the same tasks. Because of this, their blood sugar might get low. It won't be low enough to cause a medical emergency, but it will be low enough to cause fatigue, restlessness, trouble focusing, and even a sick feeling.

Moderately sugary beverages can be a solution for this. Skip soda and energy drinks. Those will be too much, too fast. But a drink from Starbucks, a sip of apple juice, or a smoothie can provide the rise of blood sugar that your teen might need. When they have these, try to keep them from drinking them too fast. That won't help, and it will cause a sugar crash.

A huge struggle that many people with ADHD face is test-taking and learning. Now, in the adult world, there might not be tests, but there will be meetings, presentations, and more that they will need similar skills for. It's important to develop these skills as early as possible so that your teen enters the adult world with a sort of muscle memory of how to get through these tasks.

Our last chapter also talks about something that is important now and when your teen gets to the adult world. Right now, socializing is how they build up their friend circles and how they talk to their elders, teachers, and those younger than them. In the future, it will be about how they talk to customers, interact with coworkers, and forge relationships in the adult world.

Chapter Eight
Building Confidence and Social Skills

When her daughter was diagnosed with ADHD at the age of seven, Mary started to prepare. She studied all of the habits associated with ADHD. She was prepared for emotional explosions. She was prepared for the difficulty that her child would have in school. She was ready for the mess. From day one, she helped her daughter with all of these challenges, and she's happy to say that it worked, and her daughter now does fine in these areas. There is just one thing she didn't see coming, and as such, she felt completely unprepared for it.

Mary's daughter, Rose, is now 14. Mary started to notice some small changes in Rose when she was 12. She was quieter. When she turned 13, Mary noticed that when she offered praise, Rose didn't quite seem to believe her. Finally, one day, when Rose was struggling particularly badly because she couldn't focus, Mary pulled her away from work and tried to remind her about some of the good things about ADHD. Rose screamed at her mother to stop before she ran to her room and slammed the door. Mary was shocked. She thought she had done a decent job in highlighting the positive aspects.

When she was able to talk to Rose the next day, she got the truth. Rose wasn't struggling with her ADHD because of issues focusing. She was struggling because it made her different from her peers. They didn't seem to think as she did, and it made the whole thing incredibly difficult. Not only that, but she noticed that she had a hard time either keeping up with a conversation or not getting ahead of it. Her friends seemed annoyed sometimes, and it was really affecting her.

This isn't something we think about when we think of ADHD, but the impact it can have is huge, especially in the teen years. With ADHD, this can also become a hyperfocus issue, and if that happens, it can affect them well into adulthood. The teen years are a time when self-esteem is especially vulnerable as well.

Because of ADHD, social skills can be harder to pick up. It can be harder to read the room and focus on a conversation. This can affect how people perceive a person, and that can cause severe self-esteem issues. On top of that, we have to think of the effect of ADHD as a label. Positive talk at home may only be able to do so much when the world is a cruel place. For that reason, this chapter is dedicated to the social and emotional effects of ADHD and how to combat them.

Tips For Developing Social Skills In Teens

Guidance In The Moment

Guidance is especially helpful when your teen is younger (though it works at any age). You likely often see your teen interacting with others and working. You might notice when things are off with their behavior and when it doesn't fit into social situations.

When you notice this, pull them aside. Gently go over what they did and how it didn't fit, and then advise them on a better strategy for next time. Try something like, "Hey, I was watching you talk to that person, and when they were telling a sad story, you tried to make a joke. I know you were probably just trying to lighten the mood and make them feel better, but instead of doing that, it actually hurt them and made them think you weren't listening. Maybe try some words of encouragement?"

This isn't going to be a comfortable talk for your teen, so managing your tone and trying to make them as at ease as possible will help with the reception of the information.

If you notice a lot of issues within a short time period, it might be a good idea to make a note and talk to them right after the event instead of during it.

Roleplay

Your child might struggle with specific situations. If they come to you with troubles or if you notice them, suggest a roleplay. This can give them a chance to walk through different ways of responding and help them get a chance to practice and test out different behaviors. The next time they need to deal with this specific social situation, they are ready and know how to handle it appropriately.

Facial Expressions

Facial expressions that come naturally to you might not come so naturally to your teen. There are a couple of ways to help with this. One method is the use of facial expression charts. Elementary children often use this when they are first learning, and it can be incredibly helpful for children with ADHD as well.

Another thing you can do is watch TV with your teen and point out different facial expressions. Going back to behavior, you can also use TV to demonstrate actions that are appropriate and actions that aren't.

Goal Setting

Goal setting is helpful in dealing with a lot of issues that are the result of ADHD, including social situations. A goal can look like paying close attention to a line of conversation, being more empathetic, or making sure that others also have a chance to speak. Help your teen find measurable ways to achieve these goals and then set them.

Give Them A Lot Of Opportunity To Practice

I understand that there is a certain temptation to have them stay home as much as possible when they tend to have issues with social environments, especially if those issues lead to emotional explosions, but we are all trying to raise our kids to be successful adults, and that will hurt them in the long run. Doing the opposite is actually going to be more helpful.

Get your teen used to social situations and proper cues. The more they are able to get out and practice and work on it, the better off they will be in the future.

When you are looking for different things to try with your teen, look for things that will interest them. Find conferences and conventions for their hobbies. Have them join sports and clubs that they like. Find groups that cater to their interests. All of these will be engaging so that social practice doesn't feel like a chore, and it will provide practice for social engagement.

Play To Their Strengths

Each brain and each case of ADHD is going to be different. There are going to be some things that they do really well and some things that they will need to work on. As they navigate these challenges, they are going to hear a lot of feedback about the things they need to work on, and that feedback isn't always going to be kind. If you find that after an event, you're going to have to talk about a lot of things that went wrong, try to add some balance. Throw in things that they did right as well. Not only does this help delivery and prove that you're not just watching their mistakes, but it also provides positive reinforcement.

Another thing that might help is finding an outlet for their more challenging behaviors. If you notice, for example, that your teen tends to be opinionated and tends to try and argue with relatives over a difference of opinion, suggest they join a debate club. This is an outlet that will give this ability a chance to have an outlet, and they can learn a lot at this club, including more social skills.

Talk To Them

This one seems so simple, as we talk to each other every day. But, how often do we sit and have a conversation with little to no distraction?

Invest in the time to do this with your teen as much as possible, or at least once a week. It will help them with these skills, and as they get older and when they do grow up, you will be glad you set aside this time.

Talk To Them About Sensitive Topics

When someone is struggling with ADHD, it can be hard to sort out their thoughts on big topics.

At the time of writing this, news headlines are lit up with major controversial topics, and that's unlikely to change at any point in the future.

With so much news on highly charged topics floating around, your teen might have trouble sorting through all of their thoughts on these issues.

Sit down and ask them what in the news stands out. If there are a lot of things, have them write them down. Then, ask them about their feelings, followed by their thoughts. Give them space to work through these, and try not to influence them to think one way about something, as it can make it harder on the brain.

Practice Their Listening Skills

This is a big one. It can be hard for those with ADHD to actively pay attention to conversations, even if it's one they are involved in. It can also be hard for them to stop talking, especially if their brain gets on a train of thought. Try to both model this behavior, and give them gentle reminders when needed.

When someone has ADHD, they are capable of many things, including big ideas. This serves them well in the adult world so long as they are able to communicate their ideas.

Social skills can be a lifelong learning process for everyone. It's easy to blame that needed learning on ADHD interference and let it hurt your self-esteem. The teen years are a point where your child might be especially vulnerable to this, and that can carry to adulthood. How do we prevent it?

Tips To Help Your Teen Boost Self Esteem

Self-esteem gets more important the older your teen gets. Low self-esteem is tied to issues with self-worth, as well as mental health issues such as anxiety and depression.

Because of their brain's issue with dopamine production, people with ADHD are already prone to mental health struggles. There are steps that can be taken in the home to help!

Be Mindful Of Self-Talk

Self-talk is your inner voice. How you think about yourself and the words you would use to describe yourself is a part of self-talk.

When we have negative self-talk, we tend to put ourselves down. We might ignore the good qualities we have and put way too much emphasis on qualities we see as being bad.

You might notice that your teen has negative self-talk if they seem to either talk a lot about themselves using negative language or if they make comments like "I'm not smart," "I'm useless," or "I can't seem to do anything right."

If you notice this about your teen, try to work on positive self-talk. Affirmations can be a great way to encourage positive self-esteem. Another thing you can try is reframing. If your teen makes a negative comment about themselves, have them stop and rethink it. Rephrase the statement in a way that encourages positive self-talk.

Is Your Teen Kind To Themself?

One thing that your teen is going to need to remember is that they have ADHD, and because of that, they might have to do twice the work to get the same result as their friend. When they accomplish something, they should be proud of themselves that they were able to get that result.

What might happen a lot of the time is that they are upset because the extra effort feels like a reflection of their ability. It's not. Teach your teen to celebrate their victories, acknowledge that some things are going to be harder, and celebrate when those things are taken care of.

Have Patience

When your teen gets frustrated with themselves, try to use strategies to steer them toward a more peaceful line of thought. Your teen might expect the same results that everyone else gets from the same level of effort. Remind them that it's okay to have patience for yourself. It's okay if things take a little more effort.

Don't Make a Habit Of Comparing People.

Do you notice that when they are struggling, your teen might say something like, "all of my friends do fine with this material." or "they are able to control themselves in class with ease. I can't do that."

When you see that, make it a point that everyone is different, or point out things that they do really well that others can't.

If they compare themselves to others, they might end up in a battle with their self-esteem.

Our teens are growing human beings that are becoming adults very soon! With adulthood comes certain social graces and having the confidence to get through the world.

Review

Hi there, I hope you enjoyed the book and got some value from it!

If you did and thought it will benefit someone else then please spread the word and leave a review.

If you share the book and it brings value to others, then they will be so grateful to you and you will feel great for helping another person struggling with the same problem.

Many thanks, Kenneth

Free Gift

Please pick up your free gifts. I know how tough it can be dealing with emotions, so I have put together a parent's guide to dealing with emotions just simply scan the barcode below, and you follow the instructions to access your free copy. There are also two free ADHD printable planners you or your kiddo can use.

Conclusion

It can be hard to think about your teen heading into the adult world. Not only are they your baby, but they also have ADHD, and you still see some struggles.

Hygiene, which we talked about in chapter one, is one such struggle. Your teen might be putting it off to the last second because of issues with focus, sensory troubles, or thinking that no one is going to care. In the first chapter, we talked about several strategies that can help this process.

Along with proper hygiene, there is the need to keep the body healthy. If the body doesn't want to work, then neither will anything else. It also can be a preventative measure for severe ADHD symptoms. In chapter two, we talked about diet, exercise, and cooking healthy meals.

If your teen is still struggling with emotional control, you might be very worried about them moving out. Part of emotional control is making use of resources around you, like a 504 plan. There are also strategies that you can use in the meantime to cool off.

Another aspect of both the teen and adult world is organization and time management. Both of these might look different to someone with ADHD. They will need different methods and strategies, but when they find something that works for them, then that is something they should stick with!

Impulsivity might become an even bigger issue when money gets involved. In chapter five, we talk about impulsivity with money and ensuring that financial decisions are made with intention. We also talk about how to set up a visual budget with ADHD.

In chapter six, we discussed home and adult life maintenance. There are many things that we don't even think about as teens that involve home and paperwork. Knowing how to take care of these things can save a lot of hassle down the road!

Finally, the issues of memory, confidence, and social skills are handled in chapters seven and eight. These are considered soft skills, which are always best to be taught as soon as possible. They can help make your teen's adult life easier, and it helps them on their journey in both their teen years and their adulthood.

ADHD or not, your teen is going to go on to do amazing things. With your help, they will have the skills they need to get by.

References

8 Successful people with ADHD you should know about. (2020, January 22). University of the People. https://www.uopeople.edu/blog/8-of-the-worlds-most-successful-people-with-adhd/

19 Activities for kids with ADHD that burn energy and improve focus. (2018, November 26). Meraki Lane. https://www.merakilane.com/19-activities-for-kids-with-adhd-thatburn-energy-and-improve-focus/

ADDitude Editors. (2016, November 28). Famous people with ADHD. ADDitude. https://www.additudemag.com/slideshows/famous-people-withadhd/

ADDitude Editors. (2020, March 25). Kids bouncing off the walls? These boredom busters fill time gaps with activity. ADDitude. https://www.additudemag.com/bouncing-off-the-walls-activitiesadhd-kids/

ADHD and behavior - tips on how to discipline your child. (n.d.).

Supernanny Parenting. Retrieved May 19, 2022, from https://www.supernanny.co.uk/Advice/-/Parenting-Skills/-/Discipline-and-Reward/ADHD-and-behaviour-~-tips-on-how-todiscipline-your-child.aspx

Allen, S., & Psy.D. (2020, March 31). "Our home can't withstand all of these emotional ADHD explosions!" ADDitude. https://www.additudemag.com/adhd-control-emotions-parent/

American Academy of Child and Adolescent Psychiatry. (2019).

ADHD & the brain. Aacap.org. https://www.aacap.org/AACAP/Families_and_Youth/Facts_for_Families/FFF-Guide/ADHD_and_the_Brain-121.aspx

Anderson, J. (2021, April 13). The effect of spanking on the brain.

Harvard Graduate School of Education.

References

104

https://www.gse.harvard.edu/news/uk/21/04/effect-spankingbrain

August 11, G. M., & 2020. (2020). How to help kids with

attention and learning issues with remote, hybrid, or in-Person learning. Parents. https://www.parents.com/health/add-adhd/how-parents-can-helpchildren-with-attention-and-learning-issues-with-remote-hybrid-orin-person-learning/

Brown, T. (n.d.). ADHD and emotions. Www.understood.org. https://www.understood.org/en/articles/adhd-and-emotions-whatyou-need-to-know

Brown, T. (2016, November 29). Exaggerated emotions: how and why ADHD triggers intense feelings. ADDitude. https://www.additudemag.com/slideshows/adhd-emotionsunderstanding-intense-feelings/

Carpenter, D. (2006, October 6). Never punish a child for behavior outside his control. ADDitude. https://www.additudemag.com/behaviorpunishment-parenting-child-with-adhd/

CDC. (2019, August 27). Other Concerns and Conditions with concerns and conditions associated with ADHD. Centers for Disease Control and Prevention. https://www.cdc.gov/ncbddd/adhd/conditions.html

Chronister, D. K., & Program, K. T. T. T. (2021, June 19). Best activities for teens with ADHD Key Transitions. https://keytransitions.com/activities-for-teens-with-adhd/

Cohen, M. (2018). Can you treat ADHD without drugs? WebMD. https://www.webmd.com/add-adhd/childhood-adhd/can-youtreat-adhd-without-drugs#:~:text=Exercise

Crawford, J. (2018, April 25). Parenting tips for ADHD: 21 ways to help. Www.medicalnewstoday.com. https://www.medicalnewstoday.com/articles/321621#twenty-oneparenting-tips

Facts about saturated fats: MedlinePlus Medical Encyclopedia. (2020). Medlineplus.gov. https://medlineplus.gov/ency/patientinstructions/000838.htm#:~:text=Saturated%20fat%20is%20a%20type

ADHD Raising an Explosive Child with a Fast Mind 105

Healthline. (2013). What are the three types of ADHD? Healthline. https://www.healthline.com/health/adhd/three-types-adhd

Kessler, Z. (2013, October 26). The secret to no-shout, no-tears discipline. ADDitude. https://www.additudemag.com/discipline-withoutyelling-calm-parenting-for-kids-with-adhd/

Kris. (2019). 25+ strategies for kids with ADHD. Pathways 2 Success.

https://www.thepathway2success.com/25-strategies-for-kids-withadhd/

Legume basics. (n.d.). Www.dvo.com. http://www.dvo.com/recipe_pages/betty/LEGUME_BASICS.php

Leonard, J. (2019, May 31). ADHD diet: Best foods, foods to avoid, and meal plans. Www.medicalnewstoday.com. https://www.medicalnewstoday.com/articles/325352#foods-tolimit-or-avoid

Marcy. (2016, November 1). How to teach life skills to your teen with ADHD. Ben and Me. https://www.benandme.com/teaching-lifeskills-teen-with-adhd/

Myers, R. (n.d.-a). 10 concentration and focus building techniques for children with ADHD. Empowering Parents. https://www.empoweringparents.com/article/5-simpleconcentration-building-techniques-for-kids-with-adhd/

Myers, R. (n.d.-b). Effective consequences for ADHD kids. Empowering Parents. Retrieved May 19, 2022, from https://www.empoweringparents.com/article/effective-consequences-for-adhd-kids/

Norton, A. (2021). Science reveals how red meat harms the heart. WebMD. https://www.webmd.com/heart-disease/news/20211229/sciencereveals-how-red-meat-harms-the-heart

Parekh, R. (2017, July). What is ADHD? American Psychiatric Association; American Psychiatric Association. https://www.psychiatry.org/patients-families/adhd/what-is-adhd

Sherrell, Z. (2021, July 21). What are the benefits of ADHD? Www.medicalnewstoday.com.

References

https://www.medicalnewstoday.com/articles/adhd-benefits#adhdsuperpowers

Tacoma, N. (2019, March 11). Mindfulness and ADHD: 4 relaxation games for children. ImpactParents. https://impactparents.com/blog/adhd/mindfulness-and-adhd-4-relaxation-games-for-children/

Watson, S. (2016). ADHD: 7 life skills your teen should master. WebMD. https://www.webmd.com/add-adhd/childhoodadhd/features/adhd-life-skills

Watson, S. (2021, February 8). 21 ways to make lemonade during the sourest times. ADDitude. https://www.additudemag.com/activities-for-kids-with-adhd-skills-pandemic/

Whelan, C. (2021, April 12). 8 ADHD meditation & mindfulness tips.

Healthline. https://www.healthline.com/health/adhd/adhdmeditation#tune-out-noises

8 Basic Cooking Skills Every Budding Chef Must Know. (2019, January 3). The ICCA Stockpot. https://iccadubai.ae/stockpot/8-basic-cooking-skills-every-budding-chef-must-know

American Academy of Child and Adolescent Psychiatry. (2019). ADHD & the Brain. Aacap.org. https://www.aacap.org/AACAP/Families_and_Youth/Facts_for_Families/FFF-Guide/ADHD_and_the_Brain-121.aspx

Bean, S. (n.d.). Poor Hygiene in Children: "My Kid Stinks!" Empowering Parents. https://www.empoweringparents.com/article/poor-hygiene-in-children-my-kid-stinks-help/

Bernstein, S. (2021). ADHD and Your Emotions: Tips to Help You Manage Them. WebMD. https://www.webmd.com/add-adhd/emotion-stress

145

Bhandari, S. (2020). Get Organized: Tips For Living With Adult ADHD. WebMD. https://www.webmd.com/add-adhd/ss/slideshow-adhd-living-tips

Brittany. (2018). ADHD & Keeping up with Hygiene, Keep Calm and Grow On. https://keepcalmgrowon.com/adhdandhygiene/

CHADD. (2018). Relationships & Social Skills, CHADD. ht

tps://chadd.org/for-adults/relationships-social-skills/
Cruger, M., & Ph.D. (2006, October 6). 15 Memory Exercises for Forgetful Kids. ADDitude. https://www.additudemag.com/working-memory-exercises-for-children-with-adhd/

Dolin, A., & M.Ed. (2016, November 28). 10 Secrets to Studying Smarter with ADHD. ADDitude. https://www.additudemag.com/slideshows/how-to-study-with-adhd-and-ace-even-tricky-exams/

Editors, Add. (2016, November 28). 13 Clutter Hacks for the Easily Overwhelmed. ADDitude. https://www.additudemag.com/slideshows/quick-cleaning-tips-for-the-easily-overwhelmed/

Flaxington, B. (2015). 5 Ways to Stop Beating Yourself Up. Psychology Today. https://www.psychologytoday.com/us/blog/understand-other-people/201505/5-ways-stop-beating-yourself

Gunnars, K. (2018, July 24). Mediterranean Diet 101: A Meal Plan and Beginner's Guide. Healthline. https://www.healthline.com/nutrition/mediterranean-diet-meal-plan

Hallowell, E., & M.D. (2013, October 24). Anger Is Important — But Only When It's Managed. ADDitude. https://www.additudemag.com/anger-management-techniques-for-children-with-adhd/

Harveston, K. (2019, December 9). 7 ADHD Mindfulness Exercises for Kids, Teens and Adults. The Mindful Word. https://www.themindfulword.org/2019/mindfulness-exercises-adhd/

How to ADHD. (2021). ADHD Friendly House Hacks - Feat.

MY HOUSE! (Executive Function Friendly Tips). On YouTube. https://www.youtube.com/watch?v=posZhu_YIlo

https://www.facebook.com/verywell. (2019). Helping Your Teen With Time Management for a Successful Life. Verywell Family. https://www.verywellfamily.com/teaching-time-management-skills-to-teens-2608794

Jackson, M. (2021, March 23). When to Keep and When to Throw Away Financial Documents. HerMoney. https://hermoney.com/earn/taxes/when-to-throw-away-Rnancial-documents/

Joanne. (n.d.-a). How Can a Child With ADHD Improve His or Her Memory? Thinking through ADHD. Letrieved June 18, 2022, from http://thinkingthroughadhd.com/index.php/2018/07/27/how-can-a-child-with-adhd-improve-his-or-her-memory/

Joanne. (n.d.-b). How Can Parents & Teachers Help ADHD Teens Fit in Socially? Thinking through ADHD. https://thinkingthroughadhd.com/index.php/2018/12/29/how-can-parents-teachers-help-adhd-teens-Rt-in-socially/

147

Josel, z. (2020, October 13). Q: "What's the Best Way to Study for a Test with ADHD?" ADDitude.

https://www.additudemag.com/how-to-study-adhd-test-prep/

Kholberg, J. (2006, October 6). Shortcuts to a Cleaner, Less Cluttered House. ADDitude. https://www.additudemag.com/housekeeping-made-easy/

Kolberg, J. (2006, October 6). 33 ADHD-Friendly Ways to Get Organized. ADDitude. https://www.additudemag.com/how-to-get-organi#ed-with-adhd/

zang, S. (2022). Cornell scientists help to develop Asian Diet Pyramid, Cornell Chronicle. https://news.cornell.edu/stories/1996/01/cornell-scientists-help-develop-asian-diet-pyramid

zuria, Y. C. (2017, October 25). What To Do When Your ADHD Child Has Poor Hygiene. Blocked to Brilliant. https://blockedtobrilliant.com/your-adhd-child-has-poor-hygiene/

Moak, D. (2021, March 12). 7 Simple Cooking Tips and Tricks for Beginners, Eating Europe. https://www.eatingeurope.com/blog/7-simple-cooking-tips-tricks/

Saline, S. (2021, February 10). 5 Ways to Reframe Anxiety for Your Worried Teen. ADDitude. https://www.additudemag.com/anxiety-in-teens-adhd-reframing-skills/

Saline, S., & Psy.D. (2018, August 22). Q: How Do I Teach My Teen to Manage Emotions? ADDitude. https://www.additudemag.com/adhd-teen-managing-emotions/

Schreier, J. (2020). Helping a child with ADHD develop social skills. Mayo Clinic Health System. https://www.mayoclinichealthsystem.org/hometown-he

alth/speaking-of-health/helping-a-child-with-adhd-develop-social-skills~:%:text=One'20of'20the'20most'20effective

Shannon, M. (2018, July 7). Hygiene in ADHD Kids: Teaching Independence. Miss ShannonUs Cat Farm. http://cat-farm.com/hygiene/

Teaching Teens with ADHD Money Management. (n.d.). Www.brain balance centers.com. Letrieved June 18, 2022, from https://www.brainbalancecenters.com/blog/teaching-teens-with-adhd-money-management

Thomas, A. (2020, December 15). 10 Easy Ways To Get Kids Excited About Cooking, According To Experts. Delish. https://www.delish.com/kitchen-tools/a34749087/10-easy-ways-to-get-kids-excited-about-cooking-according-to-experts/

|.S. Department of Agriculture. (2020). MyPlate M |.S. Department of Agriculture. Www.myplate.gov. https://www.myplate.gov/

Willard, C. (2018, March 9). Teen Stress Is Very Real — and Manageable with These Exercises. ADDitude. https://www.additudemag.com/slideshows/mindfulness-exercises-for-teens-adhd/

Wise, L. (2017, April 26). 23 Time Management Tips to Increase Productivity in Teenage Students with ADHD. Education and Behavior. https://educationandbehavior.com/studying-tips-for-adhd-students/

World Health Organisation. (2021). Healthy diet. Www.who.int. https://www.who.int/initiatives/behealthy/healthy-diet~:%:text=A'20 healthy'20 diet'20is'20essential

WriterMay 10, E. B., & 2011. (2020). Five Tips for Time Management for ADHD Children and Teens - Daily Life - ADHD. Www.healthcentral.com. https://www.healthcentral.com/article/managing-adhd-symptoms-Rve-tips-for-time-management-for-children-and-teens

www.ingramcontent.com/pod-product-compliance
Lightning Source LLC
Chambersburg PA
CBHW072046110526
44590CB00018B/3056